These layouts are precious tools for giving wonderfully accurate readings that bear powerful messages which aid you on your journey toward wisdom, freedom and a fulfilling, balanced life style. The eloquent, trustworthy and opinionated voice of the Tarot is designed to uplift your spirit and keep you moving in the right direction during times of personal crisis, change, challenge and confusion.

*Berkley Books by Nancy Shavick*

**THE TAROT**
**THE TAROT READER**

# THE TAROT READER

## NANCY SHAVICK

BERKLEY BOOKS, NEW YORK

Special thanks to Debra Street,
Ellen Kinnally and all my fine
friends in WHB

## THE TAROT READER

A Berkley Book / published by arrangement with
the author

PRINTING HISTORY
Berkley edition / May 1991

ISBN: 0-425-12736-2

A BERKLEY BOOK ® TM 757,375
Berkley Books are published by The Berkley Publishing Group,
200 Madison Avenue, New York, New York 10016.
The name "Berkley" and the "B" logo
are trademarks belonging to Berkley Publishing Corporation.

10  9  8  7  6  5  4  3  2  1

FOR
RUSSELL

This companion guidebook to <u>The Tarot</u>, the first book in this series, provides more material to help you grasp the higher metaphysical keys of interpretation to the 78 Tarot cards, depicts how different angles of meaning apply to a particular card depending on the context of the reading and presents ten Tarot spreads for you to bring into play again and again on your path toward enlightenment.

If you have already studied <u>The Tarot</u>, you are aware of the symbolic value of the cards in terms of a wide range of emotional, psychological, intellectual and universal knowledge illustrated by the Tarot deck. The definitions found in Part One of <u>The Tarot Reader</u>, "Advanced Definitions of the 78 Tarot Cards", should be used in tandem with those found in Part Three of <u>The Tarot</u>. The new interpretations give you additional points of reference to assist you in fitting the proper significance of a card into a specific spread placement where it surfaces during a reading.

Part Two of <u>The Tarot Reader</u>, "Exercises in Synthesizing the Meanings of the 78 Tarot Cards", offers examples of "Card Combinations" which show how two or three cards blend in combination and "Tarot Cards with Similar Meanings" which classifies the deck by like tone, feeling, activity and vibration. Utilize both sections of Part Two as mental exercises which increase your understanding of the total impact of a card in a reading and add to your perception of the associations between the cards which are all a part of each other.

Part Three, "Ten New Tarot Spreads", guides you through spreads which are new to readers of <u>The Tarot</u> and can be used as an extension of the system of card reading put forth in the first book. These layouts are precious tools for giving wonderfully accurate readings that bear powerful messages which aid you on your journey toward wisdom, freedom and a fulfilling, balanced life style. The eloquent, trustworthy and opinionated voice of the Tarot is designed to uplift your spirit and keep you moving in the right direction during times of personal crisis, change, challenge and confusion.

# Table of Contents

PART ONE: Advanced Definitions of the 78 Tarot Cards
THE PIPS
The Swords ................................. 12 - 29
The Disks ................................. 29 - 48
The Cups ................................. 48 - 67
The Wands ................................. 67 - 85
THE TRUMPS
The Fool ................................. 85
The Juggler ................................. 87
Juno ................................. 89
The Empress ................................. 91
The Emperor ................................. 92
Jupiter ................................. 94
The Lovers ................................. 95
The Chariot ................................. 96
Justice ................................. 98
The Hermit ................................. 100
The Wheel of Fortune ................................. 101
Strength ................................. 103
The Hanged Man ................................. 105
Death ................................. 106
Temperance ................................. 107
The Devil ................................. 109
The Tower ................................. 112
The Star ................................. 113
The Moon ................................. 115

The Sun                                          117
Judgement                                        119
The Universe                                     121


PART TWO: Exercises in Synthesizing the
          Meanings of the 78 Tarot Cards


Card Combinations                                125
Tarot Cards with Similar Meanings               130


PART THREE: Ten New Tarot Spreads


Monthly Astrological Spread                     144
Natal Astrological Spread                       145
Elements of the Zodiac Spread                   148
Elemental Spread                                150
The Chakra Spread                               151
Soul Mate Search                                153
As Above, So Below                              156
Lifetimes Spread                                157
Three Card Spread                               158
Problem/Solution Spread                         158

# ADVANCED DEFINITIONS FOR THE 78 TAROT CARDS

## The Swords

## ACE OF SWORDS

The sword suit illustrates a struggle toward knowledge, different ways of thinking and various philosophies of life. They are social cards that activate your mind and help you procure your goals.

The ace of swords in a reading can symbolize: making a plan and sticking with it; being true to your word; realizing suddenly what you must do; moving quickly to accomplish certain tasks; seeing the obvious path before you and following it; possessing enough confidence to feel capable of achievement; believing in your ability to generate positive change; becoming equal to the challenge posed by the reading.

This ace tells you to stay optimistic if you want to proceed energetically in the right direction. All decisions made here champion your own interests and give you the necessary self-assurance to unify your intentions and move forward on the clearest path to your future.

## TWO OF SWORDS

You learn to control your most subtle thoughts and maintain a positive outlook with the two of swords. Here you change your life for the better through keeping alive a mental picture which reflects the outcome you desire in a situation. This card creates a crisis of faith which tests how much belief you have in your ability to utilize your thoughts to alter your destiny. You must remain cool, calm and collected during this tense internal struggle for intellectual self-discipline.

In terms of love, this sword speaks of staying relaxed when you are without a partner and using the opportunity to center yourself minus distracting thoughts of any relationship. With the two of swords, you comprehend the wisdom of your romantic past so you know the best way to go next time. This card shows a stage of spiritual development where your mind becomes a tool for projection and the gleaning of knowledge from other realms. To accomplish this, you must slow down and become one with the pulse of life present in all creation on all levels of consciousness.

## THREE OF SWORDS

The three of swords can depict such emotional predicaments as: you want to become intimate with someone but they are not interested in you; you are feeling lost without someone; you reluctantly leave your partner with great sorrow and reservation; you love one who cannot break through their romantic problems to be with you, so you move on to look for a happier union. You may have to remove yourself from a situation by letting go of a person who is a central part of your life in your mind. This separation takes time to recover from as their companionship is sorely missed. Everything having to do with this individual makes you anxious, awkward and vulnerable and every word they say has great significance for you.

The depressive aspect of the three of swords makes you feel you have no real home or security. This can lead to states of gloom, agony, confusion and oversensitivity, all symptomatic of growing stronger through emotions that are painful for you to deal with. This card also speaks of having heavy thoughts concerning our troubled world and the incongruity and tragedy of certain lives.

# FOUR OF SWORDS

The four of swords is a time to recharge your battery that burned out with the three. You need to distance yourself from a situation to discover your true thoughts and to sharpen your intellectual skills. This can find you retreating to a place where you can work or study such as a room, studio, office or cabin. This sword represents privacy and concentration enhancing your creativity and being in an environment which enables you to strengthen your mind, body and spirit.

The decisive quality of this card helps you to mentally review the subject matter of the reading through step-by-step deliberation. You consider your next move after careful reflection upon all potential scenarios. By assessing the details, you analyze your situation through the singular awareness of your own counsel — an important stage of sword development.

This four describes the process of sitting still and detaching your mind from your body during prayer or meditation. This quiet time helps you build up positive, healing energy about yourself and leads you to having the ability to control your thought-form projections.

## FIVE OF SWORDS

The five of swords also speaks of keeping to
yourself and utilizing verbal inhibition. Here
you make all your own decisions, no matter
what other people think you should do. If
you remain silent, your mental energy will
double in strength as you sort through your
options for the future. **Discussing** your situation with others can jinx or weaken the
outcome you desire.

   With this sword, you learn to distinguish
who or what is really worth your effort and
begin to say no to people or activities that
waste your time. You gain a better perception toward those you meet in your daily
life by becoming an alert observer who
understands the shortcomings of others
without taking their behavior personally.

   In a reading, the five of swords can
symbolize: something is not going to turn out
as you expect; that you must tell someone the
score as you see it; that you have to lay down
the law to another person; how people do
things as opposed to how you do things.
This card creates one-sided communication
that alienates you from others. You must
shield yourself from those who may play

destructive mind games or always give you grief no matter what you do.

In a love relationship, this sword would picture a situation where one or both partners cannot handle true intimacy due to selfishness or an inability to communicate honestly. There could be arguments which force you to stand up for yourself or take action on your own behalf.

## SIX OF SWORDS

This sword ships you off on a graceful path of smooth sailing in your own boat where you leave a place to recover yourself in a new environment. The six brings a journey wherever it is found in a spread either in a physical or spiritual manner. This can be a psychic trip launched to expand your consciousness or travel to other lands to seek out an aspect of your past experiences which enlighten you to the dynamic purpose of your current life. This exodus aligns your equilibrium, grants you a healing on all levels and helps you to reclaim history and knowledge that belong to you.

Channels of all varieties open up with the six which provides the perfect geometry for this mental activity to develop. The six of swords gives you access to more facets of your mind and leads you to recall incidents from the past. These memories renew your original clarity and sense of direction. After you make this connection, your life unfolds with ease along a path of least resistance as you fulfill the purpose of your present sojurn.

## SEVEN OF SWORDS

The seven of swords says you must make your own way down the road of your evolutionary progress toward self-knowledge. Like the five of swords, you must follow your heart even if outside pressure forces you to attempt otherwise. The only way to recapture your individual freedom is to be true to yourself above all else. Because your own philosophy defeats collective thought, you become someone who operates both inside and outside of the system.

This card describes how your own interpretation of universal law is empowering to you as a unique, liberated entity. This relieves you of having to play it safe by assuming a conditioned role to survive.

You are released from a time period plagued
by suffocating moral hypocrisy. With the
seven of swords, you relax once certain
people and responsibilities that were a
spiritual setback for you are gone from your
life. The self-assurance this card generates
helps you to utilize psychic self-defense
against all negative energy that drains
you or confuses your positive direction.
This stage of the individuation process occurs
prior to your knowledge of the white light
of protection as a force field which prevents bad vibrations from nearing your
aura.

　　　This sword is also a card of invention,
progressive thought, abstract genius and
those who search for unique solutions to
the problems of the world. Many new ideas
come to the surface of your consciousness
here and may lead you to a project or
business which allows you to place this information before the public.

EIGHT OF SWORDS

The eight limits your mental outlook and
frustrates you as you want to initiate
plans but the outlets are not open to you yet.

You are not really ready to be set loose anyway, so nothing that you try can change your
situation. You must wait until you get past
this restless period which is difficult
psychologically and never seems to get better.
Your path will unfold in great clarity when
the proper conclusion to your unhappy and
painful isolation has been reached. Until
then, you feel stranded, abandoned or unable to ask for help. Nobody is there to
support you and this makes you desperate
when faced with roughing it out alone.
The eight of swords is a time to challenge
your helpless attitude by opening up to
people and groups who could help you organize your life.

This card can symbolize changing
your mind and arriving at a solution
you had not considered before; being released from a state of bondage through
mental liberation; discovering the truth
after being in the dark for a long stretch.
It can signal that your limitations and
difficulties are a result of karma you must clear.

NINE OF SWORDS

The grieving factor of the eight of swords is

continued with the nine where you experience an increase of intellectual sensitivity which took root with the three of swords. Awareness of your karmic role in relation to others often requires growth through pain to release anger and sorrow from within your heart.

As with the ten yet to come, this card brings weak, weepy emotional moments which catch you unable to handle the reality of a stormy situation. Your mind becomes overextended and your rest is disturbed by conflicts which have no easy answers. This sword shows that you are conscious of the psychodramas created by those around you. By tuning in to each unique behavioral pattern, you become alert to strange personality problems in others. The nine indicates people who you find it hard to cope with as they are nasty, cruel or overly critical toward you. Their words and attitudes invade your energy field unless you come to pity these individuals whose discontent illustrates their deep unhappiness.

The nine of swords warns you against taking the blame for the karma of anyone but yourself. Do not compensate for the shortcomings of another as though you are responsible for making them a better person. Your involvement with them serves as a catalyst which moves you to the next step in your evolutionary process. You must shield yourself from negativity by not getting emotionally wrapped up in the dilemmas and projections of those who are holding back the collective spiritual growth of humanity. The nine of swords shows you retreating from the battle-ground of critical competitive people into the arms of more positive loving souls. Instead of striking back verbally at any attempt to dominate your thoughts by others, you keep to yourself and stay away from individuals who remain stuck in their animal nature. This card also finds you overwhelmed by information you need to convey or complete work on. You are agonized because you have to bring every-thing together in a very short period of time.

## TEN OF SWORDS

The ten of swords finds you flipping out com-pletely. You have too much to do, too much on your mind and too many details to oversee in a situation which must be totally organized. This card suggests the problems associated with a tortuous ordeal which drains you until you arrive at a point of mental agility where you can accomplish anything you put your mind toward attaining. During this period, your mental and physical health may be sacrificed for the sake of fulfilling your responsibilities. You extend yourself more than ever before and are drained by the rigorous training this card puts you through. Though you feel broken down to the point of having no energy or mental clarity, you learn valuable lessons through the experience of this sword which tells you self-defeating thought patterns are no longer pertinent to you.

This ten describes knowledge gained by suffering great hardships. Even if you succeed materially, your heart is full of grief over a personal loss that haunts your soul. Other definitions include: unconscious tension which makes you feel you have to account for every past mistake; possession of a photographic memory or an enlightened vision that grants you total recall of akashic history; resynchronizing previous life abilities which blossom as your current soul gifts.

The ten of swords signifies the mystery and complexity of the mind and emphasizes how small a portion of the brain is actually used. It urges you to expand in awareness and reminds you that no one can ever know what another person really thinks. This sword rules communication as it depicts an ability to reach many people through your professional ideas and interests where you share your information for the benefit of everyone.

## PAGE OF SWORDS

The Page of swords has many manifestations: asking questions; receiving a message; keeping your ear to the ground; gathering ideas, knowledge and specific data; relying on rumor and offbeat informers; utilizing caution to check things out; conducting business by telecommunication; a phone call which changes your life.

As a personality, the Page can resemble: a bold, fixated, fearsome fighter who you would like to have on your side; a person who needs to confide in you; someone who is too overprotective and loses friends who feel trapped by the relationship; those who further the goals of all they meet by helping to guide them in the right direction.

The emphasis here is to make every effort to connect with others who aid your search for spiritual identity and who are receptive to the positive qualities of your

oversoul which is the seat of your divinity.
The Page of Swords can depict: someone
who watches over you and guides your destiny; strong protection around you that prevents stagnation in your process of enlightenment; not having as much free will as you
normally do because of these forces at work;
a person with whom you communicate intui-
tively on the same mind wave; receiving information from odd places and people; no
longer feeling alone or ignored, but a part
of a greater network.

## QUEEN OF SWORDS

This Queen of the air is a speaker who rules
over her own life with a bold, direct approach.
She delegates in all environments and intimi-
dates others by bossing them around which
creates a tense atmosphere filled with bad
energy. She can be a little too harsh and
difficult, but her cut-and-dried quality actually attracts people to her who like the definite,
discerning feeling that they get from her.
If the Queen of Swords symbolizes you in a
reading, she shows you being influential
through your ideas or your behavior,
having to push for your demands, arguing

your case, getting your message across, nego-
tiating a deal or working as a therapist
or counselor who influences others to change
for the better by helping them discover the
truth of their inner being.

Negative interpretations of this card
are: someone who acts innocent but is busy
manipulating people who are weaker than herself; a person who forges ties only to further
her own ambitions; a woman who is obsessed
with judging, analyzing and criticizing others
to make herself feel superior to them through
an imaginary sense of power.

The Queen of swords symbolizes the
woman without the man whether she keeps
them away intentionally or rejects potential mates if they do not match her ideal-
ized image. She can depict women who are
asexually inclined or uninterested in a love
relationship. She signifies those who repeat the emotional failures of their
mothers through isolation in an unhappy,
dead end arrangement or who, without
true family or friends, find forgetfulness
in solitude. In a reading, the Queen of
swords can indicate time alone without a
mate which you should utilize to develop
self-confidence, willfulness and the

practical application of your own mental energy.

## KNIGHT OF SWORDS

The Knights favor the company of their horses to that of their own species. The Knight of swords prefers to be constantly on the move to get where he wants to go as fast as possible. He charges through your life pushing like a maniac for either positive or negative reasons depending on the reading.

The Knight of swords has the following meanings: you think you are secure but you are really insecure; you rush through life ignoring the joy of precious moments; you do things your way and demand others follow suit; you try to run away from confrontation; you travel quickly and with great urgency; you have a mean personality; you are selfish or self-destructive; you find it impossible to come through for anyone else; you destroy all attachments by repressing warmth and emotion.

The best influence of this card in a reading helps you to reach a new level of consciousness in your journey through the air suit. It can also send you off on a trip to launch a successful tour or campaign. This card finds you urgently wanting to contact those who share your strong convictions or singularity of purpose. In terms of love, this Knight of the clouds symbolizes someone who is interested in you, but is strange about showing his feelings. He may be a persistent suitor who woos you desperately but panics and disappears if you decide you want a relationship with him.

## KING OF SWORDS

The King of swords can be a teacher of great knowledge who through the use of his personality educates those in his school or environment. The brilliance of his mind inspires others to push themselves toward a similar state of awareness. This King is an intellectual who can be found as a superior, father substitute or employer. As he is an authority, you may be anxious about his judgement of you and view him as a threat if you fear powerful male energy.

Due to his responsibility toward

others, the King of swords is demanding and controlling so he can be a successful leader. He seems severe and self-centered because he concentrates completely on his plans. This King is wonderful to have on your side as he always finds the perfect solution to all problems you are faced with.

This sword often depicts artistic people who literally or visually capture a reflection of their own process of evolution through their work. It requires strong self-confidence to produce art that covers new creative ground and moves these individuals into the authoritative position this card illustrates.

## The Disks

### ACE OF DISKS

Every ace is a kickoff of its suit, hurling you forward into action with little interference. The ace of disks begins a cycle of material change through money, value systems, the physical world as perceived through the senses, talent developed through constructive opportunities and new interests pursued which may take years to master.

Some explanations of this card are: Someone who notices your potential and helps you nurture it; the appearance of ability and how you can develop it; that you have the potential to make things happen; setting up a strong foundation for the future; a visit from somebody that profoundly changes the course of your life. The ace of disks urges you to prepare for things long before they actually occur, such as undertaking a long study prior to when you need to utilize the discipline. Though you are not really ready for anything specific yet, you are capable of acquiring knowledge in different fields of interest which will be valuable to your eventual choice of profession. This education could come in the form of jobs that are short-lived but provide you with information for use at a later date. Financially, this ace would emphasize investing for the future, receiving seed money to begin a project or getting control over assets that belong to you but are in the trust or possession of another.

The ace of disks depicts natural ability based on the seeds you sowed in the past and the ground you will cover in reincarnations yet to come. In this way, each sojourn is viewed as a journey back to earth to replant the fields of lives past, present and future where old soul gifts are resynthesized and resynchronized into the psyche and consciousness of your current life pathwork.

In a love relationship, this card finds two people building a foundation together based on patience, acceptance and equal effort expended between them. As they relax into the teamwork required, their material necessities will be gained with ease and they will be blessed with a union that grows deeper and richer through the years.

## TWO OF DISKS

The two of disks symbolizes change as found in cycles of constant movement within the universe. This rotation creates alternating opposites of energy and attraction within infinity through the existence of dualities of action and reaction as found in nature. This card has to do with lessons brought forth by enlightened people who teach of the immortality of all beings in eternal life as manifested in the human spirit through the planetary forces since the beginning of all creation. The awareness of this truth puts life in its proper perspective as a small moment in the journey of a soul as compared to the greater history of time.

This disk is customarily considered a card of travel often sending you abroad. It describes being forced to move by circumstances beyond your control to a new environment more magnetically attuned to you which would give you a higher degree of clarity and help you break the indecision which blocks your creative development. Also, as this is a disk, economic opportunities would be better for you in a location of residence in harmony with your cosmic energy which grants an increase in employment activity for you.

The two of disks signifies a lack of a strong material foundation, not having enough money, a depletion of resources, a disruption in financial growth, narrowly getting by with everyday expenses and having trouble achieving equilibrium within a balanced life style. This disk ushers in a wide range of emotions: restless uncertainty which prevents any real change from occurring, a mind occupied by non-constructive thoughts, lacking any real direction in life and having your attention waver from one person to another romantically because you cannot decide who to choose.

## THREE OF DISKS

This disk indicates completion of an activity, finishing a project or closing a deal. You may receive a commission to accomplish certain work, find a permanent resting place for your creations or procure a job which utilizes your skills. In a romantic sense, this disk denotes settling unfinished business in a past relationship or coming to a final agreement concerning financial arrangements with a partner.

This card shows your talent being recognized and developed through the help of others, so your natural gifts can have application in the outside world. Though this disk may depict you adding people or partners to your project, its success really hinges on your efforts alone. Often the three of disks symbolizes that you need more collaborators or that you should join up with a team, group, company, community or association in order to make yourself available for the benefit of others.

This three has to do with your most readily available form of skill ability and development as well as special talent which can translate creative energy into practical forms. This card represents an environment where you can work in privacy and watch your inner genius blossom through discipline. Here you give birth to art which reflects universal truths of the human spirit and is powerful for all time to all people. The three of disks also indicates silent workers who labor toward the huge task of educating and enlightening others through constructive channels which interpret the material world in a balanced manner.

## FOUR OF DISKS

By the four of disks you can bring together any project you wish and become stronger and more capable through the process. Beyond the three, the four goes on assisting you to gain in self-confidence by helping you apply the best methods for stable success in the world. You are in a position to maneuver your own advancement without losing any assets, ground or seniority. This card often symbolizes being approached for a job by people already established in business.

This four shows money and possessions being of enormous importance to you where you prefer security over taking risks or exploring the unknown. This sense of ownership can describe a love relationship where you hold someone tightly without letting them have a life of their own. In the best of all alliances, both partners constantly improve through a mixture of togetherness and independence. Another interpretation of this disk applies to the physical body where, through relaxation, you sink into your corporeal self and become more connected to the earth.

## FIVE OF DISKS

The five of disks is a direct reaction to the preceding four: it emphasizes freedom from possessions and living more on the edge materially. This can imply being deprived or underprivileged economically, surviving hard times, being financially broken by a monetary disaster or conserving for the future. This disk depicts: being judged by your wealth or lack of it; having riches but hiding the fact; assuming a simpler life style; doing things cheaply; purchasing essentials only; tempering your consumer mentality. This card shows that if you had the proper funds you could proceed with a particular plan for skill, business or spiritual development. The highest aspect of the five of disks is when you realize that your values are programmed by societal conditioning. You learn to be more conscientious about how you use things and become more comfortable with a state of simplicity, less clutter in your environment and a halt to the creation of future money karma for yourself.

Here you become a material orphan who worries about having enough money, protection from the elements and being all alone in the world without connections. People of the five of disks are often homeless, impoverished or undercover for personal reasons or they are those who are elevated from the burden of earthly needs by being taken care of through divine providence.

## SIX OF DISKS

The economic scenario of the six of disks shows you receiving exactly what you need because you deserve it. Money always comes to you with this card and as it depicts others aiding you, it suggests you exchange whatever you can. Here your core desire is to utilize your assets for personal success but also to enrich the lives of those with whom you work or share material responsibilities. If you have given generously in the past, the time arrives for others to come through for you. You need to yield to the law of give-and-take in life which spreads opportunity all around through charitable reciprocity.

The aura of cooperation that surrounds this disk leads you to choose partners who possess the skills or resources that you do not have and are therefore perfectly suited to you. Joint ownership, either personal or professional, is described by the six of disks where equality and sharing between two people is required. Similar values join together this team that respects the principle of fairness and balance in their material relationship.

## SEVEN OF DISKS

Natural growth is the key theme of the seven of disks. This can apply to the period of development of talent that precedes a harvest of skill ability or staying with a person to see if they come through in practical terms. You know that it takes time and effort to get a garden to flower properly. This card challenges you to let your assets mature slowly by investing in your future according to a responsible life plan. Similar to the six of disks, the more you are willing to work toward a goal, the more you will benefit ultimately. The rewards of the disk world come to those who sacrifice their energy to build themselves a more fruitful tomorrow.

The main requirement here is to use self-restraint to allow for a gradual ripening of your creative capabilities. During the seven of disks, you make all the necessary preparations for your eventual material destiny. Be positive and protect yourself against self-doubt by staying busy with all facets of your personal growth. Often this card leads you to a new life style as you transfer your attention from a halfhearted attempt at completing work to a more solid, disciplined approach.

## EIGHT OF DISKS

The tradition of the eight of disks is work-in-progress where you gain in ability through practicing certain skills to make your dreams real in the material world. It always implies training through actual physical expenditure on a craft. You learn to direct your subconscious by repeating tasks which reinforce your expertise deeply in your mind. By working with your hands and creating through manual labor, you get more in touch with your sense of spirit and become more self-sufficient with your needs. You stop asking others to take care of you and make the necessary moves to get more control over your life. This eight describes wanting to be a better person and due to this having to exercise a vigilance over your personality to keep negativity out of your words, deeds and thoughts so your soul can serenely advance in its chosen field.

In terms of career, the eight of

disks represents a job you love or finding the best way to serve the world through your talent. Creatively, this symbolizes channeling your emotions and impressions into an art form. You record your feelings in visionary work made manifest through hands-on involvement with your medium to become a more capable artist. This card urges you to expand your technical knowledge and seek out master crafts-persons with whom you could serve a valuable apprenticeship.

## NINE OF DISKS

You live a life of plenty without material worries with the nine of disks. This card lets you enjoy your possessions instead of being weighed down by them as burdens. You are capable of acquiring what you need, but first you must feel capable by having total faith in your own ability. Your self-worth is highly developed because your work is special and sophisticated. You can request the payment you rightfully deserve for your effort due to your quality creations. Your inspiration is dependable and

offers of employment come to you because
of your reputation. You are finally in a
position to use your talents to channel
art that is rich in love, beauty and
aliveness.

Great treasures are yours as well as
a wealth of goodness and well-being.
You are appreciated for your true self
by others and now that you have an
audience, you are inspired to become
even more productive. Other resources
of this nine include: financial success or
independence; living life to the fullest;
having all your actions be self-explanatory; being secure about your chosen life
style. This disk also builds strength of
character and brings out the best in
you through your relationships with
other people which are based on mutual
respect and your desire to heal the
planet rather than add to the forces of
destruction.

## TEN OF DISKS

As a card of inheritance, the ten of disks
has multiple interpretations ranging
from the ancestry of your biological

family to the figures of history whose lives you emulate as positive examples. It defines your relatives in your current incarnation who you chose on the spirit side of life for specific reasons. In a reading, the ten describes your similarity to your kin through tastes, values and beliefs; guardians from whom you acquire moral, material or spiritual ideals; carrying on a line of tradition; working with a family member or love partner; being assisted financially by your relations. The ten of disks indicates money karma where you partake of resources gained through the efforts of those who preceded you. If you benefit monetarily from a business that exploits the earth and its people, this card can haunt your conscience or stunt your development as an evolving soul. You must become more responsible for your own needs or your limitations will mirror those in your family who have failed to achieve a balance in how they acquire and use things.

When the ten of disks represents you, it says: you can generate your own tradition to pass on whether roots of wealth or a beloved set of ethics; you have to spend money to make money; you become

involved in the project of a lifetime; you are
going to establish your own home and family.
Here you discover true happiness through the
practical aspect of your relationships and
deep fulfillment in your daily activities.
This card also describes the karmic nature
of all ties, brief and lasting, where you come
to understand how your soul blends with
or retracts from other souls during your
solitary spiritual journey. This awareness
accounts for this ten being a card of a
life rich with multi-layered significance
if observed through the eyes of eternity.

## PAGE OF DISKS

The Page of disks is always up-front with his
intentions and offers his talents, service,
possessions and practical assistance to
get what he wants for himself or another.
He is sincere but youthful and you need to
be slightly patient with him as he is a
hard worker once he starts moving. This
Page can aid your own development by
influencing you to apply your energy more
diligently to your own pursuits.
    Traditionally, the Page of disks de-
picts writing or expressing yourself through

the written word. It suggests you scrutinize all communications or get something down in black and white. Scholarly work is always a part of this Page who indicates you must complete your homework, go to school or study a subject. This card makes you focus on an area of interest which creates a sense of direction in your life. You are prepared to toil long and hard on a project which will reveal the ideas, values and aesthetics inside of you.

In a love relationship, this card illustrates two partners who work at their bond every day with the desire to create a happy, flowing friendship. Both people expect a lot from each other in terms of respect, mutual caring and unconditional support and affection.

## QUEEN OF DISKS

This Queen labors endlessly to help people recognize their own talent, give birth to their wealth of ability and be healed of confusion and lack of purpose in life. She is a good, peaceful and generous woman who never asks anyone else to take care of her in any way because her main concern is assisting everyone to reach a level of personal fulfillment.

The Queen of disks appears in many guises in the world: businesswoman, philanthropist, teacher, cook, farmer, doctor, scientist, geologist, astronomer, botanist, herbalist, astrologer, counselor, healer, mother, wife or anyone who works with their hands to create objects of beauty and necessity.

This disk person is a caretaker of the earth who is never exploitative for personal gain. She is more grounded than most people in her physical body, more free, more secure and with a keener sense of relaxation than the usual woman as found in a strictly patriarchal world.

## KNIGHT OF DISKS

The Knight of disks needs to be close to nature in a secluded environment, not distantly in the country, but not in an atmosphere crammed with people. A location closer to the earth grants him greater physical ease and mental clarity because he is more attuned to land than asphalt. A peaceful place brings out the best in him and there he can find fewer problems with those around him in his daily life.

By tradition, the Knight of disks is a farmer, worker or essential service person who takes care of people. He may be a naturalist who worships the perfection of the seasons which transform the planet, cycle after cycle. In the business world, he is totally responsible but he enjoys his work more than the King of disks. He has a sense of humor, romance and adventure and is more down to earth than most expect him to be.

Your life is safe in his hands because this Knight is the best friend and protector you could ask for. Your connection with him is basic in its simplicity, unity of feeling and purpose due to his being a provider who is honest, devoted, deliberate and always comes through for you. His practical mentality and temperament leads him to quietly make decisions for the collective good. When you meet the Knight of disks, you are immediately attracted to him because he is shy, kind and without pride. If you are lucky and the chemistry is right, you will discover a magical union which grows deeper through love, trust and similar values and life goals.

## KING OF DISKS

This King is warm, generous and protective as
are all the disk court cards. He watches
over you in a big way and provides assistance
to you if he considers you part of his family.
His guidance enables you to take on more
material responsibility in your own life.
The King of disks is often self-employed
and trains apprentices to carry on his line
of work to keep a tradition alive. He may
be in a position to supply security to you
through useful advice, wealth or good
connections. He supports you without hesi-
tation if he has confidence in your ability.

The King of disks implies that the
wherewithal to get your plans going will
be available to you. You are ready to:
make money, have money and handle
money; take responsibility for your work
and actions; have practical wisdom
about the proper use of the material
world; have a conscience as you build
your assets; and respect the customs of
a family or business. You may have the
opportunity to join up with someone already established in your field who has
information which prepares you for your

future.

## The Cups

## ACE OF CUPS

The cup suit represents soul energy, psychic ability and celebration on an emotional level. The sacred waters of the cups are a force of healing, cleansing and purification. The ace of cups symbolizes the first step in true intimacy with another person in a love relationship you decide to let grow. This can be the initial meeting where the words spoken or look exchanged sparks immediate attraction and sets the tone and theme for the purpose of the connection in the lives of both partners. If you are already attached, this ace grants new awareness to the existing union and finds you falling in love with someone all over again or having a reunion with one you have known previously. The happiness and excitement this generates quickens the pulse of life within you and makes you care more for the world around you. During this blissful time, you evolve at a heightened pace as everything becomes more meaning-

ful and precious to you. All sensations experienced here are positive, vibrating with
passion and gentleness of soul. As this is a
card of deep devotion, the ace says the
other person who wakes up your life is genu-
ine in their feelings and could be the one
you have been waiting for to set your heart
into motion. This ace also speaks of joyful
friendships with kindred souls who respect
and understand the true you who dwells in
the temple of your spirit.

The ace of cups indicates your potential
for psychic experience which unfolds through
the following cup cards. Do not neglect
self-protection by blessing yourself in
the light and giving thanks for your divine gifts which utilize your emotions as
a tool of intuition, sensitivity and extrasensory awareness in order to glean
knowledge from other realms. The best
way to shatter any obstructive negativity
which prevents your connecting to this
source of spiritual wisdom, is to feel the
white light of healing guarding you, ever
present through you, surrounding you
and spreading upwards through your
entire being and affecting you positively on all levels.

## TWO OF CUPS

The two of cups continues the theme of giving birth to love begun with the ace. It suggests a sweet, tender relationship where two people experience deep contentment when together. This couple has only pure intentions for each other and their sole expectation is constant respect between themselves. This type of union is selfless because true friendship exists where both individuals break through all fears and allow their emotions to flow between their hearts. These creative partners make a positive contribution to the world by sending out good vibrations to those around them.

The spiritual bond indicated by the two of cups offers you an excellent foundation from which to build up a romantic love based on mutual passion. If you have not met your special person yet, put out your need for someone sincere to enter your life who will be totally intent on you and with whom you can share a serene and enjoyable home life. If this card finds you in an established union, it could represent you and your partner renewing your vow of commitment. The two can also symbolize bonding in spiritual realms where your oversoul responds to natural psychic communication with another seat of intelligence.

## THREE OF CUPS

Get ready to have fun with the three of cups: loosen up and express the joy of being alive; relax by escaping the drudgery of material demands; celebrate good times, close friends, parties, weddings, happy news and rejoice over there being an abundance of treasure to share. On a more serious level, this three brings great victory in that you attract like-minded people to you with whom you share moments of spiritual solidarity of purpose. These connections inspire you to stay on the high road with a certainty that you will reap the tremendous reward of eternal cosmic gold.

The three of cups helps you to break through to a wider range of emotional expression. Also, your psychic gifts increase through exchanging perceptions with others in positivity. Your intuition is keen at this time and can be used to help people understand the truth behind the drama of their lives. In love, this card indicates that you are ready for a workable relationship just a step beyond the ace and the two of cups. You want to taste the fruits of a union which celebrates aliveness, sensuousness and playfulness and be part of a couple who enjoys the cornucopia of pleasure which nourishes the soul.

## FOUR OF CUPS

The offer inherent in the four of cups is always exciting and enticing but may not really be right for you. You should perhaps reject this opportunity and instead follow alternate plans or hold out for something better in the future.

Emotionally, this card shows you unavailable for a new intimacy because you still remain in love with someone from your past. Your social life no longer seems attractive as you have difficulty finding anyone suitable in the circle around you. The four of cups depicts romance as a distracting quantity where you replay scenes of encounters over in your mind which disorients you in your daily life. If this card depicts a solid friendship instead of relationship stalemate, it symbolizes the highest level of stability in a strong, monogamous union between two equally serious people.

During this time, you weary of your routine and feel out of it, bored, absent-minded and lack the ability to concentrate. Avoid getting involved with anyone or anything new until you can organize your passionate self to utilize meditation and relaxation as natural outlets to build up positive creative energy. Stay peaceful and powerful in an attempt to ascertain the wisdom of your attachments through use of your superconscious channel which contains all you have seen, been and known and can only be tapped through absorption in the abstract.

## FIVE OF CUPS

The five of cups illustrates falling in love with someone and the relationship not working out. You remain emotionally un-fulfilled by the experience though you attain greater self-awareness through the ordeal. Though the connection was a disaster, you must give your passionate nature another try in the future for the cups that are still standing. The loss can manifest in the breakup of a romantic tie that was not fruitful. Due to soul imbalance or karmic interference between you and another person, it would be better to move on alone. When one partner cannot meet the ideal of the other, failure and disappointment permeate the union though an attempt should be made to salvage the friendship if possible. Perhaps you are deluded about the true availability of the other person and are wasting your energy on someone who does not share your feelings.

Other interpretations of the five of cups are: feeling left out and let down; losing something or someone; frustration; discouragement; a cancelled date or event; feeling alone in the world. This card makes you seek higher ground emotionally and reclaim your serenity and contentment through acceptance of your current life reality. You must try again at achieving personal happiness without fear of being hurt or betrayed by others because you view them through fanciful projections of your own hopes and dreams.

## SIX OF CUPS

This six invigorates you through a rebirth of generosity, a rejuvenation of your physical body, a renewal of inspiration and revitalization of a friendship. The emotional force of this card makes you feel like a child who is bursting with excitement and fascination for all simple pleasures and who spreads joy and happiness to all those around them.

The six of cups brings a wash of harmony, innocence and gentleness over your entire being. It gives you another chance at attracting love to yourself due to your radiating good energy out to the world. This cup projects positivity and sharing that can destroy bias, hatred and prejudice which poisons society and perpetuates tension and estrangement between groups of people.

This card indicates enjoyment of an innocent sensuality with one partner who reciprocates your feelings. The relationship is constantly energized by an emotional exchange that is balanced in mutual attention and devotion. This cup also speaks of a past union being re-established in a new light where both people sincerely want to give it another try.

## SEVEN OF CUPS

As a card of expansion, the seven of cups symbolizes: wanting more than you can have; approaching a problem by viewing the big picture; completing the necessary preparations to fulfill your destiny; getting a mental glimpse of the future; realizing what is deeply satisfying to you; procuring your dreams through the visionary cup world. In any case, you must keep your options open and examine the entire field with a wide perspective before you narrow down your scope to what you can realistically develop.

The seven of cups represents activation of your creativity through the proper use of your imagination where you choose from a myriad of ideas, interests and activities that attract you. You explore the one or two chosen pathways that give you the greatest potential for success in this incarnation.

Creative visualization is strong with this card and brings results in your life. For an artist, this would indicate the arrival of inspiration which can be translated into rich concepts and imagery in your work. For the spiritualist, the seven is heaven: your intuition opens up; the future can be seen through prophecy and clairvoyance; you can use your psychic abilities to inform people of their eternal soul history. The seven of cups suggests a knowledge of previous lives through visual and emotional recall of details locked in the memory of the collective unconscious which surface through dreams, fantasies, astral travel and the power of unseen worlds of intelligence.

## EIGHT OF CUPS

The eight of cups makes you determined to acquire that which deeply satisfies you. You leave behind the superficial traps of the cup world that dissipate your emotional strength and enter a stage in your spiritual evolution where you are ready for the soul challenge of initiation into the mysteries. You feel you have a larger goal in life and yearn to study metaphysical ideas in a private environment. To gain strength and purify your karma, you need to give up activities that waste your energy and take up a more creative direction. This card suggests prayer, devotion, vigilance over your own personality, following your inner voice and surrendering to the divine by moving to a higher plane of adoration.

If the eight of cups represents an intimate relationship, it shows involvement with someone who is worth your effort and who is dedicated to causes of the spirit. You want this person to be a large part of your life and if mutual passion, sincerity and commitment hold you together, you could be in for the long haul with each other.

## NINE OF CUPS

With the nine of cups, you find self-satisfaction, eternal happiness and serene contentment. You stop generating negative karma to have to deal with later on. Your sense of well-being is due to finding your proper social expression through refined friendships which are eternal ties rich in unconditional love. You experience a deep, unspoken dialogue with one particular person with whom you create a miraculous connection between your hearts and minds. The nine of cups reminds you that there is someone in this world who was born to love you and when they appear in your life they are attracted to your real self, not your mask. A wonderful security develops where you feel complete when together and any games are unnecessary because this is a long-standing, highly evolved union that continually grows and handles all crises with love and positivity. You receive a great deal of sympathy, affection and understanding from this soul mate who is always there to meet you with open arms.

## TEN OF CUPS

The ten of cups brings success to your life in financial, intellectual, passionate, emotional, social and especially familial terms. This card is a key to joy, peace and stability through a happy marriage, home or family which connects you to a community. This ideal arrangement is too rarely found but is a constructive formula for attaining some level of enjoyment in the midst of a shattered society.

The tens are maturations of their suit which in the cup world denotes a relationship that develops naturally without preconceived expectations. Any difficulties facing the union inspire both people to seek eventual happiness for all involved. You hold the well-being of your friends and family above all else without allowing trivial troubles to cloud your rightful serenity. You welcome those who make a sincere effort to get close to you. Your lifetime becomes a positive experience due to the aura of loving protection around you. By the ten of cups, your will power has evolved to the point where you only have the purest desire for a complementary social life where you can achieve a perfect balance of feelings and behavior.

## PAGE OF CUPS

All cup people are intense, abstract and overemotional; all Pages offer themselves to others. The Page of cups is: open and available; a nice person who has only good intentions; not picky, snobbish or a complainer but sympathetic and loving; attracted to new people and experiences; a youthful admirer; a devoted and trustworthy confidante; a sociable person who enjoys parties and gatherings.

In love, the Page is sweet and heartfelt in his intentions. He is totally caring and always ready to give you everything he can. If he is attracted to you, you will know it, because he does not hold back his feelings. The Page of cups easily shows affection though he may be afraid of getting hurt by you which is not grounded in reality but based on a past romantic pattern. He may function on a subconscious psychological level and be unaware of the archetypal role he has designed for himself to play. Another facet of his personality is a desperate need to always be with the one he loves because he fears her leaving him.

In the highest sense, the Page of cups is a happy person who helps others relax their guard long enough to enjoy the playful, childlike part of themselves. In a reading, this card represents the child in everyone who longs to surrender to warmth, tenderness and closeness with their lover and explore sensuality through a relationship which builds trust between himself and his loved one.

This Page has artistic ability which results from his natural response to beauty and sensation. He is a dreamer who seems lost in his imagination where he creates unique work which finds its own appreciative audience.

## QUEEN OF CUPS

The positive side of the Queen of cups would emphasize her calm, intuitive, compassionate heart of gold which she extends to anyone in trouble or in pain. She is not prejudiced and knows all people are one through similarity of instinct and the goal of soul development. She can be found as a responsible artist, charity worker, volunteer or selfless activist who promotes life and fights neglectful predatory forces in the world. She is a sympathetic humanitarian always able to understand and accept the shortcomings of others.

Her most mature trait is that of forgiveness as she is capable of turning new corners every day and releasing the past from herself.

The negative forms of behavior of this Queen would be a nebulous quality where she changes her mind because she is fickle or confused about what she wants. She may be too generous with people who tend to suck her energy dry and use her for their own advantage. She can be naive or trustworthy to the point of gullibility by setting herself up to be drained by others. Adding to the fog surrounding her would be any self-destructive tendencies if she slips into debauch through excessive use of that which fills her cup.

In a reading, this card symbolizes: offering love or physical assistance to someone; being hard to pinpoint; not forcing any issue but having faith that the proper outcome will occur on its own; stepping back to witness the drama of your destiny unfolding; exercising your psychic ability; being in an easy love relationship which you float along through without making a commitment. Often this Queen represents the "other woman", a female who is emotionally dominated by their partner and a woman who chooses an older or more experienced mate for guidance and stability in her life.

## KNIGHT OF CUPS

As do all the cup court cards, the Knight offers love to those who fill his cup. He will follow you anywhere as long as you continue to provide the stimulation he needs. Do not expect his interest in you to match the intensity of feeling that you have for him. Any proposal from him should be considered inappropriate, irresponsible and impractical. Though the emotional inducement is there and the spiritual attraction is there, he should not be a permanent man for you. Even if the match appears ideal, you would ultimately become miserable if you remain attached to him. The Knight of cups is unreliable and untrustworthy to the extreme and never comes through on his intentions he words as promises to you. You must decide whether he is worth pursuing as his treating you like a second-class citizen is not right for you. Perhaps you should seek a more secure man who desires the type of relationship you do. This Knight would suit you only if you enjoy abuse from those with whom you share your love.

The Knight of Cups can be sexually immature but tries to prove his prowess through promiscuity and dissipation. He has little self-respect or self-protection and never seems to be serious about anything. He has a terrifying subconscious fear of being honest, intimate and dependable with another person. As a love interest, he is the sort who woos you briefly with great intensity and then never calls again. His staying power is short because his romantic urges are purely physical or active only in his deluded imagination and pass as fast as all impulses do. He is hesitant and indecisive about maintaining any ties and may never have a long-term connection with another in his life.

## KING OF CUPS

This King often shows up in a reading to indicate a powerful or prominent man with an aura of charm and mystery to whom you feel psychically pulled. He may be far away from you but he is still intensely interested in you. His emotional reserve makes you assume he does not like you because he is not with you: this is not necessarily true. He does not share his feelings prematurely to anyone even if he wants to. The taciturn King of cups can be connected to wealth or one who pretends he has nothing due to paranoid money madness. He can be hiding a mental or substance abuse problem about which the Knight of cups would be totally up-front.

The King of cups is the card of love distracting your from your work. Daydreaming about this person interrupts your concentration and disrupts the growth of your talent by taking energy away from your true purpose. To complicate matters, the inaccessibility of this King makes you more romantically preoccupied with him. Because you are in illusion over him, you become awkward, ridiculous and humiliated when you are with him. The King of cups dominates all his relationships and expects people to come to him and play the role that he has chosen for them.

Unfortunately, the King of cups is usually harsh or negative in his behavior. He can be a tough employer who treats you badly or rips you off; a withdrawn, sullen man; an unsmiling, ruthless businessman who is difficult to deal with; a competitor who is trying to get the best of you. He can be testy, abusive, unfriendly and even cruel because he functions on an unconscious level of insecurity. He has trouble resolving his antagonism toward everyone who approaches him and is exhaustingly complicated and difficult to easily understand.

More mundane descriptions of this card are: remaining silent regarding the matter of the reading; a deal is definately in the picture for you; you are extremely attracted to a project or business venture; that someone is not speaking up or a message is not getting through.

## The Wands

## ACE OF WANDS

A new day dawns with the wand suit

where you start afresh and move ahead with energy, excitement and confidence toward the future. You begin a cycle of action and growth utilizing invention and innovation to approach untouched territories of experience. Whatever enters your life with the ace of wands inspires you to meet the opportunity it represents by preparing for what is yet to come.

You must quickly accept the challenge of this ace. You can handle what is happening because of your strong desire to undertake pursuits of interest that you have not gone forward to try before. You may go off with the most unexpected companion who positively charges your battery through the fire and the passion they bring into your life. This relationship revitalizes you and refreshes and purifies your soul. This card also represents the holy spirit, the original spark, the primordial flame and the electrical current which give birth to life as well as the powerful explosion which begins and ends all cycles of creation.

## TWO OF WANDS

The two of wands forces you to take command of your life without expecting anyone to help you. To establish your identity in the world, you must go out and place yourself in a position to be noticed by others who can help you join the club of interest you need to be a part of to succeed in your chosen field.

This card requires you to have strong determination to reach more solid ground so you can become the master of your own destiny. You must consider the far-reaching prospects of all your actions while at the same time taking the initiative to move further along your path.

With this wand, you get to a point in your development where you can control your creative inspiration and utilize your talent and resources for the best of all artistic purposes. You may have too much positive energy and ambition with this card but it takes extraordinary self-confidence to achieve the recognition that comes with the three of wands.

## THREE OF WANDS

By the three of wands, the work that you
watched over with great passion is complete.
You have achieved extensive self-knowledge,
mature artistic ability and now know the
creative influence shall always dominate
your outer world pathway. This card
often requires you to become more responsible about developing yourself to the
fullest in this lifetime. It suggests your
creations will bear messages that will
receive strong reactions from your audience.

Due to a preoccupation with potential opportunities, you may neglect people who have saved or enlightened you in
the past. During this time, you should
reactivate the old relationship and seek
out those from your past to remind them
how much you honor them. Make an
energetic social effort to establish caring
exchanges with those you meet in your
day-to-day activities and expand your
circle of friends. Romantically, the three
of wands alerts you to your own feelings
about someone and reveals your passion
for them. Once this card passes, you can
proceed to woo them with an open and eager

heart.

## FOUR OF WANDS

This card symbolizes your right to joy and happiness whether you want to settle down in a satisfying living arrangement, a harmonious relationship with a loved one or a place of peace and contentment. This is an important developmental phase of your creativity where your life is enhanced by the comfort of a warm, serene and beautiful residence. This is a shelter you dearly love and are always joyful to return to after you are away from home. In a reading, this card indicates you will find a spot on earth attuned to your planetary energy that aligns you with happiness and heralds a spiritual homecoming.

The four of wands welcomes people into the room and is a social card whereby you can act as a peacemaker in your community who offers a neutral environment for opposing groups who need to gather and communicate in an effort to heal rifts and suspicion between them. This card speaks of the necessity for compromise, cooperation and friendship in order to enjoy the fulfillment of a group of people whose bond is based on mutual trust, decency, survival and a high level of respect amongst themselves. A stabilization of your passionate nature occurs here because you surround yourself with strong personalities who provide leadership and support for all your endeavors.

## FIVE OF WANDS

All risks associated with the five of wands are worth it because you are challenged to choose a way of life that implies a struggle from which you emerge victorious with the six of wands. You cherish ideals for yourself and the world and make a commitment to help find answers to the problems that prevent the rising up of the collective consciousness of humanity and the healing of planet earth. This is an important point for you to reach and you may be inspired to go out and win support for a cause or issue in a teamwork situation. You become additionally spiritually responsible through your activism and must remain positive so your original purpose does not get distorted or hypocritical during entanglement with those of opposing views. The arguments that erupt with this five help you sharpen your debating skills against anyone who tries to undermine your efforts. This card speaks of competitive people, especially in a work and business situation, and implies an ego struggle for the purpose of developing individual free wills.

Some manifestations of the five of wands in a reading are: being irrational, having a bad attitude, wasting your time, hating something in others you really hate in yourself, feeling an urgent need to overdramatize your life, feeling suspicious of your own desires, having lots of energy, dying with excitement over someone or something, getting involved in a fiery spontaneous love affair, building yourself up through physical exercise to increase your overall strength and not giving up on a relationship that is going through an up-and-down period.

Psychologically, this card shows rage directed at the parents or other relation who hurt you previously. This anger is deeply embedded in your psyche and personality and keeps loving people away from you who might help you get past this self-defeating defense mechanism which stunts your creative and passionate growth.

## SIX OF WANDS

The long fight suffered through the five of wands is won with the six. The victorious breakthrough of this card affects every area of your life and represents what you want to do more than anything and that you are willing to risk all you have to get it. Your self-confidence in your creative ability increases with this personal triumph as you are rewarded for your effort and commitment to your goal.

Due to the exalted feelings that accompany this wand, you are pleased with all relationships symbolized by this card. Your passionate self shines with optimism and lofty ideals of love and friendship. You are eager, ardent and sincere about establishing a fulfilling union with a partner who has values and an emotional maturity that complements yours perfectly. If you are already attached to the person of your dreams, the six of wands shows how the ultimate prize in life is true love with one who sets the path of your heart into motion.

## SEVEN OF WANDS

The seven of wands reminds you to stick to your plans and not let your attention waver in a particular situation. Do not procrastinate taking action even if you have to fight on your own behalf to stay on top. It is tough to go it alone, but you cannot give up or lose hope with this card. Stay aware and keep anyone and everything away that distracts you from your goal. This is a time to utilize a high morality, so be sure your intentions remain honorable and that you never resort to low behavior. If you have to deal with unpleasant people you do not like, you may need to put more effort into your situation with them so your connection can reach a swift conclusion.

In terms of imaginative work, the seven says you are proud and talented but

at a low point of physical energy. Your well
of inspiration often runs dry with the seven
of wands and you really have to force your
intuition so your creativity can flow stronger for you. You attempt many projects
here but are never quite satisfied with
the results. Though you are not fully
developed yet in your field of interest,
you must keep yourself involved in the
artistic process so by the ten of wands
you are more mature as a productive
and capable craftsperson.

## EIGHT OF WANDS

There is always great confusion, quicken-
ing and speediness with the eight of
wands as though you are jet propelled
into movement. You must accomplish an
enormous amount in a very short time.
This card, like the seven, challenges you
to take action and can make you panic
due to the overwhelming choices of ways
to go. It indicates something will happen sooner than you think or shows you
counting the days until an exciting
event in the future.
   Travel is often symbolized by the

eight of wands: the necessity for leaving immediately on a journey, going cross-country or abroad, satellite dispatch communications and astral navigation through a higher level of existence. Spiritual inspiration is available with the eight as well as an increase in vital force, creativity and sexual energy which heals you on all planes of your being through a resurgence of cosmically charged particles. For the artist, this represents a rush of unreal, perfect and exciting ideas and imagery which become source material for your work.

The eight of wands depicts being taken by surprise in love. It shows someone suddenly appearing out of nowhere who forever changes the course of your life. Their arrival wakes you from your coma of being unloved and their devotion makes the blood flow stronger through your body and livens up your heart and soul.

## NINE OF WANDS

This card indicates a strong, positive force at work which supports you

in all your endeavors. You can easily extend
yourself into any situation due to your
self-confidence which naturally leads
you closer to your goals in life. You must
stay centered and determined, keep your
head together, guard your privacy and
place yourself in a protected position
with the nine of wands. Once you build
up the proper foundation of character,
you can succeed through your sense of
purpose, developed ability and desire
for stability.

   You may have to control and inhibit
a powerful physical force through your
strength of will with this card. It
often describes feeling ready for something but having to wait until the right
time at a later date. In order to remain
dedicated to the tasks at hand, you
need to put off people and things that
waste your precious energy and weaken
your efforts to be in command of your
life.

   To lay down roots with the nine of
wands, you must seek support from
places and people who were not acces-
sible to you before. These sources will
now assist you to create a protected

shelter for yourself, escape dead end situations you find yourself stuck in and give you the self-confidence necessary to choose more constructive activities and relationships in hope for a better future.

## TEN OF WANDS

The ten of wands shows you ready to do anything to make something work out even if it means carrying a heavy load of responsibility for yourself and others. As this burden bogs you down, it becomes increasingly obvious that you have not signed up for easy. You are paralyzed by how much you have to do and though you are overwhelmed, somehow you manage to get it together. With this ten, you generate an overload of energy which can fry you with too much electrical current and push you to seek, fight and gain through the experiences brought into your life with this card.

Romantically, this wand speaks of being extremely serious about a commitment to another person. You hold a very heavy torch for them and have no doubts about sharing a future together. If you are unattached, the ten of wands represents the weight of being unloved or throwing yourself frantically into activities that substitute for a real relationship. In a creative sense, this card is indicative of possessing talent but not knowing what to do with it. If you do not actively develop your natural ability, you will forfeit this opportunity before your skills have had a chance to grow.

## PAGE OF WANDS

The Page of wands is a socially interesting person who is enthusiastic about adventure and living life to the fullest. He finds joy through a youthful curiosity and is a born follower in search of a leader or a guide. His devotion, innate trust and inspirational support moves him to seek teachers to instruct him in areas of interest he finds compelling and wants to explore.

In a reading, the Page of wands symbolizes: being true to yourself; staying detached but friendly during

a rough period in a relationship; moving
ahead into something new without hesi-
tation; being the life of the party who
holds the attention of a group of people
together; becoming the central force
behind a project that would fall to pieces if
you departed.

The Page of wands is very passionate,
enjoys companionship and is refreshing to
be with as he does not have a jaded
personality. His caring makes all the
difference in the lives of those he feels a
kinship with; when in love he is faithful to
the extreme and always makes the
happiness of his partner his main
concern.

## QUEEN OF WANDS

The Queen of wands has a high-spirited
and volatile exterior but beneath her wild-
ness lies a pure heart. She represents the
energy of womankind and to her feminism
is a natural right which enables her to
avoid being victimized by anyone. She is
creative in her own right and takes control of her life by breaking through the
oppressive conditioning which limits the

privilege of women to be free. To achieve her
goals in a patriarchal world, she is extra
demanding and has to believe in herself
even if nobody else does. This tough,
vital and independent Queen champions
her own interests and is self-reliant in
all her affairs and because of this she
arrives at a powerful position of passionate integrity.

As an artist, the Queen of wands
is inspired by the wisdom and value
of her own experience. She is naturally fiery and this quality attracts ad-
mirers to her who appreciate her
creative talent. In a reading, this
card shows you being truthful, imaginative and outspoken by crafting original
work which may be controversial but
is a manifestation of your most cher-
ished dream.

## KNIGHT OF WANDS

This Knight signifies a healthy hunger
which can be much too strong and needs
to cool out a bit. Your libidinous feelings
lead you to rank desire above importance
in terms of your romantic involvements.

The lesson of the Knight of wands is to stop and examine your impulsiveness in a relationship where the other person is probably superfluous to your true direction, so it would be best to leave them out of your life. If not, this individual will distract you from concentrating on your ultimate purpose because they are too unstable to provide the security necessary for a permanent alliance.

This Knight symbolizes someone who pursues you for weeks and then disappears without a word. In love, this card means: someone is running from commitment; a short-lived passion; a lover who physically leaves you; fearing intimacy; preferring empty, casual relationships; being afraid to act out your desires; ignoring your true feelings.

This card can indicate the necessity for departure from a situation. It moves you to a new environment, perhaps one you will like better than your current location of residence. This Knight shows you traveling for reasons of great urgency or having to change your direction quickly and race away from a potential challenge. The Knight of wands can also portend someone approaching you with a plan or a mission that sends you out into the world to fulfill its purpose.

## KING OF WANDS

The man represented by the King of wands is a blazing star of light who radiates good energy to you and makes you happier and more alive when you are with him. He is a sweet, trusting man who only wants the best for you. He generously offers his advice and assistance in a kindly way. Though he believes in you, he cannot fully support you in all areas of your life. If this King does choose to go for you, it would be too good to be true but more often than not he is primarily involved elsewhere. He makes an excellent business partner as his affable personality attracts people to him. This card has been known to represent the top person in an organization who makes all final decisions but is unavailable to you at the time of the reading. His eventual judgement of the output of your work will determine the future direction of your career.

The King of wands usually has an important outer life persona and may be prominent in the world. He always seeks to improve himself through honesty, faithfulness and responsibility to his passionate nature. Though everybody is drawn to his purity, this King pursues romance with one carefully chosen person whom he desires mentally, spiritually, emotionally and physically. In a reading, he often describes a married man, a spiritual connection or a platonic friend who brings fire into your life. If you are in love with him, be prepared to share him with others who need his reliable, positive friendship or you may lose him if you try to control his social life.

## The Trumps

### THE FOOL

The infinite spirit sparkles with the first trump which sends you on a journey in consciousness undertaken through the following twenty-one trumps. The Fool frees you from past obligations once your karma becomes balanced enough so you can begin metaphysical studies with a positive viewpoint. This movement is usually initiated by a particular vision or revelation which establishes a new integration of force which is highly beneficial for you. You undergo an actual change in body cells which ignites a total joy of life and gives you the freedom to follow a path of enlightenment through your current incarnation. With the Fool, you are in an adolescent stage of your spiritual transformation which will be complete once you have traveled the distance to the Universe, the final trump card.

The Fool must constantly be reminded he is of the earth. He lives an unfettered existence because he finds bliss in not having to deal with material burdens. He is seen as an iconoclast by a consumer-oriented society where people fear his lack of interest in ownership. Though the Fool takes his truths and values seriously, he maintains a sense of humor toward certain appetites of others and this makes him appear slightly mad or idiotic to the large percentage of the world. Many

are jealous of his freedom and his seeming
absence of obstructive Karma. The Fool
describes the divinity of those who commune
with unseen intelligence: a prophet, visionary or ecstatic through whom natural
telepathy and synchronicity of sensation
help him to find wisdom and knowledge
in the lessons evoked through the supreme
symbolism of conscious and superconscious
everyday events.

The Fool in a reading depicts the
following: avoid sticking with a specific
plan and just let things be; be idealistic
and open yourself up to new avenues
which may take you further to the edge
than ever before; in love, adopt a wait-
and-see attitude and allow a relationship to spontaneously develop without
formulating a conditioned role for the
other person in the drama of your life.

## THE JUGGLER

In the most positive sense, the person represented by this trump is very experienced and
only lets certain people into his private world,
if they pass his test. The Juggler may be a
secretive type or one who understands

natural forces as they regulate the patterns
of earthly life through a deep knowledge of
how these mysteries came forth from the
heavens. He can recall a time when humanity had mastered planetary energy and he
lifts the veil held over these truths to those
who are really ready for such sacred information. He has a solid, spiritual reason
for his behavior in order to keep pure his
ability to delineate cosmic force as it
manifests through the planes of earth
and the soul of the universe itself.

In a reading, the Juggler shows a
heavy metaphysical connection between
you and another based on the unseen. With
this card, you are never certain what the
other person is up to because all their
moves are intentionally prearranged.
This individual hides everything in order
to increase his power through manipula-
tion of reality so he can obscure your
image of him. This trump also shows you
at a high point of optimism and confidence where you become more of your
own person. Once you realize so many
great spiritual gifts are revealed only
in private, you learn to use time spent
alone to strengthen the force of your own

free will.

## JUNO

Juno relates to heavenly energy as it manifests in the light of the infinite spirit and
the ability to utilize the delineation of
this force for insight toward discovering
the cosmic nature of earth and its people.
With this card, you attain a life style where
you can live out your divinity which liber-
ates you to follow your true purpose. This
trump represents an old soul who has
worked in past incarnations in certain
fields of interest so in this lifetime these
inherent soul gifts come quite naturally
and should be applied for the benefit of
healing the wounds of the planet and humanity.

When Juno depicts this part of you
opening up, it reminds you not to over-
intellectualize your instincts due to a fear
that others will judge you. Instead, relax
your mental function and allow transmissions of information from above to
become a part of your cellular con-
stellation. Listening to the guidance of
your own inner voice will help you to

recognize your own subconscious genius.
If your mind is anxious or overextended, the
vibration of lightness will be distorted.
Once you attain ease with this aspect of
yourself, the love and wisdom you receive
will be hard for you to contain.

In a reading, Juno shows you with
your element of creative fire in balance
with your experience of emotional water.
Due to this, you are able to tune in to the
akashic records and read the story of the
history and mystery behind each soul
through the language of ancient wisdom.
This ability and awareness allow you to
bear messages for others about the karma
generated through good and bad choices made
life after life.

Juno brings forth: dreams, prayer,
divination, readings, prophecy, revelation,
clairvoyance, telepathy and all other forms
of tapping the collective unconscious which
can be used to connect people psychically
to their higher selves.

The ageless sacred sciences find
application today through Juno-type
occupations such as: healer, occultist,
herbalist, priestess, poet, visionary artist,
astrologer, channel, mystic, psychic,

card reader, oracle, therapist, wise woman or trustworthy friend who helps you affirm your divinity. The careful and considerate women of Juno know the world and can predict its ways by applying ancient information for the spiritual benefit of the advancement of the human race.

## THE EMPRESS

Where the more solitary Juno is often abused, misunderstood and even rejected by society, the feminine energy of the Empress is more generally accepted. Her potent physical force makes her sensually receptive to tasting and enjoying the gift of life. This is an important stage in your healing process where you play with the fruits of the earth which are not decadent but meant to nourish the body and the spirit. With this trump, you yearn to establish a hearth and home where you can meet all daily responsibilities with love, ease and content continuity. The Empress shows you with a partner who admires you and feels blessed to reside in a positive atmosphere where family and friends are never a drain, the enemy or competition.

You extend humor, empathy and affection to all who look to you for maternal tenderness.

In a reading, this card shows a woman who takes care of herself and others, is often treated like a queen by those around her, lives in a community that respects her and feels secure with her own femininity. For a man, the Empress finds you in touch with your gentle, compassionate side. It can symbolize a strong creative force that connects you with your feminine intuition and makes you receptive to a variety of visual, emotional and intellectual inspiration. This trump can represent a mentor or matriarch who oversees the nurturing of your talent. The Empress describes the Goddess as relative to womankind and the workings of the spirit which give birth to light, harmony and balance in eternal life.

## THE EMPEROR

During the Emperor, you discover how best to serve a situation by pulling yourself together to achieve a leadership position.

This card requires you to be instantly strong and mature but remaining gentle and caring toward those who see you as a figure of authority. You may be an executive with employees, an elder in your community or a spokesperson who people depend on to have a voice and a sense of direction. You rule with wisdom and dignity creating specific laws to insure that all people are treated fairly and with equal respect. You maintain sterling relationships based on honesty and dependability which facilitate your accomplishing great tasks of organization.

The Emperor can signify someone who watches over your development on a practical level and who may be set up to aid you financially. He teaches you rational expertise in a certain field of interest so you can strike out on your own or start a business, secure a home and lifestyle or become an entrepreneur. His conduct sets an example for you in terms of the necessity for making the best possible choices so you can attain usefulness in society and be in control of your work and your life. In love, the Emperor depicts a stable partner who is always there for you. The foundation of his soul force is clear, responsible and grounded and he is one who was born to be a monogamous mate due to his deep desire for a solid, workable union.

## JUPITER

Jupiter is native to the ninth house in the astrological chart and is ruled by the ninth sign of Sagittarius in the zodiac. Jupiter and Sagittarius symbolize teachers, study groups, foundations, institutions, spiritual centers, schools, bookstores and communities. At the heart of this trump is the right to choose your own personal code of values and beliefs based on religious freedom for every individual as you move forward in your evolution. Benevolent Jupiter lets you observe the world in a deep philosophical way through comprehension of the symbolism of everyday events as your destiny unfolds. To ascertain the wisdom of your life and times you must suffer through lessons and make choices that are neither easy nor trivial.

This card emphasizes an accumulation of awareness about divine law as well as being able to tap into the great akashic archives where images, languages and people from the past define the millenniums of now forgotten sacred art, science and mystery. Through the force of this card, familiar tools and skills of a trade are reintegrated from previous experiences and found in your consciousness during your current sojourn.

Jupiter shows a strong chemical attraction between souls who form an eternal karmic bond and return together each lifetime to challenge each other toward spiritual growth and responsibility. You are always on the lookout for a transcendent relationship with another above and beyond what most people have and are willing to wait for the appearance of the right partner.

## THE LOVERS

This is a very passionate card that brings love to you in many forms and indicates your purest desire which is to have a relationship with someone who has romantic ideals that match yours. The Lovers shows you experiencing an immediate mutual attraction with another person who you remember from a past life together. You meet your soul mate when the time is right for both of you to work out shared karma from long ago.

This is the trump of love, courtship, marriage and choice of a partner. It speaks of a friendship in its earliest stages before reality invades the situation. This type of union remains unchallenged by any crisis that would test the true nature of both people. A personal decision is always part of the Lovers because the spouse you choose will influence the course of your life. Therefore, be certain and careful not to form a bond with someone who is just a passing test and not a permanent fixture around you. Once you find your rightful partner, you experience a close rapport you have only dreamed about until that time. This love sparkles with intensity, intimacy and a total desire for and commitment to each other.

## THE CHARIOT

The Chariot signifies the power of observation

and tells you to keep your eyes and ears open so you miss nothing. With this card, you are given time to wait, watch and witness your own development without any anxiety concerning the future. You need to slow down and stand apart to witness the distinction between poignancy and urgency in all situations. You come to see the drama of your life as small exercises which add to your awareness of that which feels beyond your control and comprehension.

The Chariot represents fast forward motion which involves departure on a journey to an energy center on earth where you experience a revelation or a miraculous occurrence. Other interpretations of this card are: being absolutely certain about something, wanting to succeed in your field, making good use of what you already possess and staying neutral so you can emerge victorious in any struggle.

If the reading is concerned with love, this trump lets you know that your soul mate will seek you out and literally be brought to your door when you are ready. Until then, relax and enjoy the wonder of your own spiritual evolution through creative activity and calming meditative states. Looking back later on, you will see how all past relationships fit into the pattern of your heart during romances which precede your most perfect of unions.

## JUSTICE

This trump shows how your behavior needs to be balanced through your range of thoughts and deeds. You must account for the past, present and future of your soul which makes your life easy or difficult, depending on your reactivated karma. Your personal history holds great clues to the reason for your current incarnation which is designed for you to achieve equilibrium and outgrow misery and peculiar situations which seem terribly unfair and beyond your control. You need to trust spiritual law above earthly law and uphold a moral code that guarantees your freedom and your ability to create your own future. The eternal divine conscience of reincarnation teaches you how to persevere in removing obstructive force from within you which leads you to project negativity into the lives of others. The goal here is to protect your own dignity through the choices you make so you can be in tune with your spiritual origin as a child of the universe.

The inheritance of this trump is one of karma passed down through the generations as children repeat the mistakes, failures and personal loss or creativity, happiness and privilege of the parent most identified with psychologically. This drama also conveniently mirrors your pre-birth problematic tendencies and gives you an early start at confrontation with the issues facing you this time around. Your childhood, be it sad or joyful, is designed to help you release this burden from yourself through the close proximity of relatives to whom you react strongly.

Justice does represent the legal system and warns you: against tempting fate with authorities; to be protected legally through lawyers, contracts and agreements; to form an alliance or dissolve a partnership; to argue out a dispute over which you can only hope for a fair verdict. A decision is always reached with this card which will give to you or take from you depending on what you deserve. If you have handled your material responsibil-

ities honorably through positive and selfless
service, you receive the gift of divine
reciprocity which fulfills your every basic
need and helps you hold your future in
your own hands.

## THE HERMIT

The Hermit is an isolated card that keeps
you separate from others so you can experience the solitude crucial for psychic
development. You need to search within
your soul through meditation to gain the
wisdom and spiritual value of what is
happening in your life. After a confusing
or painful period, you step back, pull
yourself together and get in touch with
your deepest thoughts. To spend quiet time
alone, you retreat to a place where you
can slow down and concentrate on self-
knowledge. You seek out a Hermit-type
refuge or sanctuary where you can open
up to the will of the infinite spirit and
receive guidance which helps you set
realistic goals for yourself based on
absolute principles. You find a room of
your own, an office or a studio where
through privacy and distance you can

focus your mind without interruption on the work at hand. Sometimes the Hermit shows a change of residence or a journey to protected sites such as a valley, forest, mountain top, cave, island, cove, boat or tower.

This trump can also indicate joining a spiritual group or scholarly enterprise because you want to grow closer to the truth through the study of a tradition. Someone may knock at your door who instructs you creatively and philosophically and guides you back to your highest purpose.

Sexually, this trump can symbolize an introvert, celibate or aesthete who is detached from their own physical passion. In a love relationship, the Hermit is always prepared to move on alone if their partner does not meet their standard of perfection.

## THE WHEEL OF FORTUNE

The Wheel shows good things coming to you beyond what you currently expect: more money, happiness, awareness, contentment and opportunities for

expansion arise with this card. The
Wheel of Fortune always says you will
be blessed with luck you do not know about
yet. This trump challenges you to take a
chance and jump on the great carousel of
destiny where you move in perfect timing
through material gain or growth in consciousness. Success is inferred from
this card, so you must organize yourself
to be prepared for the extra responsibility which is the positive development
that evolves through the Wheel.

In terms of astrology, this trump
symbolizes the blueprint of your destiny
established in soul form through the
natal horoscope which is created from
geometrical calculations based on the
moment and place of your birth and
how your chart relates to the ever changing movement of the spheres as they soar
through the constellations of our galaxy.
The elliptical band of the zodiac helps
define continual cycles of eternal time and
change marked by sojourns to earth as a
celestial soul. In a reading, the Wheel
could denote transiting planetary aspects
which are heavily responsible for the
twists and turns of your fate. This card

has to do with places on earth where a chart is derived from the moment of establishment of the town and how its horoscope corresponds to your natal, progressed or relocated chart. The Wheel also highlights forces of duality in nature which oppose each other as complementary counterbalances such as: life and death, day and night, light and dark, hot and cold, wet and dry, rise and fall, creation and destruction and all other material polarities.

## STRENGTH

This forceful trump gives self-discipline to those who are ready for it. Strength fortifies your character and helps you fight your lazy, negative, complacent, thoughtless and even evil tendencies. You clean up your mental and physical health with an unshakable perseverance at removing insecurity, self-loathing and a sense of worthlessness brought forth through imbalanced experiences in your past. The emotional issues which still trouble you are left over from previous lives and your childhood background. These conditions are further complicated by any alienating dependency on artificial intoxicants. Often someone enters your life who inspires you to undergo purification through the power of will. Your attraction to them helps you re-evaluate your activities and choose moderation in all your appetites. Strength describes taking complete command of your inner power to get free of all substances that make you vague out and reinforce negative Karmic blocks in your personality.

The card of courage is also symbolic of being prepared for coming earth changes as we approach the beginning of a new evolutionary cycle. You have to respect the ultimate power of our slowly changing, self-healing planet where earthquakes, tornadoes, volcanic explosions, floods, climate extremes, the breaking up of continents and the shifting magnetism of the poles are all part of its history. Strength shows you seeking out a more self-sufficient life style where you put more effort into procuring your physical necessities instead of passively paying others to take care of your requirements. This new living arrangement will move you to a place where you can reside closer to the earth and its resources.

# THE HANGED MAN

With the Hanged Man, you become more conscientious of your behavior in order to undertake the most positive path through the experience of your lifetime. You may have to sacrifice one person or thing for another that is more nurturing of your spiritual growth. You must surrender completely to a new commitment that reflects what is best for you rather than what you would like to do at the time of the reading.

The Hanged Man depicts total devotion and unconditional love where you act through obedience to a principle which represents the highest fruition of your soul purpose. Others may become threatened by your nonconformity because their status quo cannot embrace you on your quest. When you embody a divine law your self-service is a natural outgrowth of being in tune with the themes and issues of your current incarnation. Align yourself to this truth and you will be able to overcome any obstacles you may encounter. The consequence will be an increase in creativity, opportunity and the inspiration to help others work toward the great goal of collective enlightenment in a time and place where all people can live out their own spirituality.

In a reading, this card symbolizes causes of the spirit, charitable individuals, holy persons, guidance counselors and those who have mature values and sympathetic wisdom that helps you attain the highest work to be done on earth involving the evolution of your soul.

## DEATH

The Death card describes moving through different stages of development in life and casting off outdated physical versions of yourself as your body and your personality mature. A deep healing is underway with this trump which creates new soul substance in you through total transformation. This card is one of radical change where outmoded forms of appearance and behavior leave your being and then you are liberated to mature into the next cycle of growth. You emerge from this transition as a butterfly freed from the protective cocoon of the Hermit who rises toward the sunlight from the sheath of what used to be.

Death is representative of the history of people and the planet where bone, wood, stone, shell, artifacts and ruined settlements are the only relics of the ages which give clues to any recall of previous lives and times. These more permanent substances survive the millenniums and are physical evidence that can be used to chronicle the ancient past. This card indicates communication with noncorporeal beings, disembodied spirit guides, out of the body experiences, the world of astral travel and near death incidents which offer glimpses of the immortality of the soul.

This trump always says something is over and describes devastating loss where nothing in your life remains untouched by its force. This can manifest as: death of things and associations no longer pertinent to you; alterations in your ego; fear of the future or fear of death; dread that someone will leave you who defines your existence.

## TEMPERANCE

This Tarot card shows you becoming a whole

person through mental, physical, emotional and spiritual healing which rejuvenates your entire body and improves your overall behavior. During Temperance, you concentrate on achieving physical health and well-being through convalescence which mends wounds of the embodied self as well as those of the soul. This trump finds you helping others temper their personal extremes by applying your knowledge of the sacred arts which assist in the release of negative karma or by sending out simple, positive and uplifting thoughts and prayers to those in need.

Before you can be of service to others, you must unify the secure and powerful aspects of your personality with the purity of your soul. Your thoughts and feelings need to undergo internal growth so you can begin to regulate and balance the fire of your mind and the wetness of your emotions.

Temperance speaks of developing your creativity through strong self-worth which gives you the faith to experiment artistically even if projects you work on take years to complete. With this trump, your life becomes your art and your art is only as original, intuitive and visionary as you are. To be able to receive transmissions that vibrate with divine intensity, you must temper all fanaticism and seek a more mellow, centered approach.

In a reading, Temperance denotes: memories fading into the past; learning to live more in the present; having to wait out a delay for your plans to be successful; being at one with the natural rhythms of day, night, sun, moons, stars, tides and extremes of seasonal lulls and storms.

If this trump denotes a journey, it guides you to power places along the surface of earth where cosmic energy manifests through lay currents which mark consecrated ground.

## THE DEVIL

This card illustrates difficulties that you were born to confront due to the interference of negative soul force which prevents you from evolving into a better person. This creates feelings of worry, anxiety, inadequacy, insecurity, states of depression or a complete lack of physical energy.

This block prevents your true character from shining forth and is based on a karmic condition carried over from the past life into the childhood experience. This trump also speaks of releasing all anger and resistance within yourself so you can move forward toward the destiny your soul has chosen for this incarnation.

This unfortunate state of being distorts your vibration and colors your aura which makes people react not to you but to your karma. This attracts those to you who fill a role which enables you to act out these behavioral problems. If you fail to liberate yourself from the weak aspects of your character which your personality oddly protects and perpetuates, you will have to repeat lifetimes ad infinitum until you straighten yourself out. This card specifically depicts the essence of what inhibits your soul from moving toward the light. And as negativity creates disease in the mind, body and astral sheath of the individual who drags their problems into a following life, so it needs to be resolved and then released through the healing power of love.

The strange emotions of this card include: fear, rage, guilt, revenge, jealousy,

insanity, delusions, paranoia or feeling de-
graded or debauched. You become chained
to a predicament which indicates your
subconscious attraction to neurotic people
and oppressive situations. Remember, this
is a self-imprisoning card where all limi-
tation is self-inflicted and self-enforced.
The personality tests are heavy with this
trump which urges you to let go of destructive tendencies which kill off opportunities
for spiritual growth. The suffering you
undergo here will ultimately lead to wisdom, enlightenment and liberation from
imaginary ties of material conditioning,
blind desire, driving ambition and being
trapped by a life style which chooses
glamour and illusion over solid values
and real substance.

The Devil symbolizes people who
behave strangely and have motives hidden
behind their intentions. Be self-defensive
through use of the white light when con-
fronting those who emanate bad energy
and try to control or poison the lives
of others. This card speaks of a social
structure based on servitude and mis-
treatment of many so the system of
slavery continues for the benefit of

the ones who make others do their dirty
work. This trump is also symbolic of emotional
blackmail where you want someone for your
own advantage - not for love alone - and
are willing to fake anything to snag them.

## THE TOWER

The Tower breaks through the lies and hypocrisy of the last card with the liberating
power of the truth. You open your eyes to
the realization that you can choose a new
way of life based on the sudden developments
that accompany this trump. The illusions
and restrictions in your environment crum-
ble away due to the emotional catharsis
of the Tower. When you are ready to recall
traumas and memories from your past,
they will surface from deep in your psyche to seek the light of day. No fantasy
lasts through the reality that is harshly
thrown at you which is designed to
wake you from the fog of mental daydreaming. When the air clears, you discover all
your self-created nebulousness prevented
you all along from beginning a clear path
to future days better and greater than
you can anticipate at the time of the

reading.

The Tower always brings a twist to any situation and shocks you with exciting, unexpected news and events where every ruined plan leads you closer to freedom. This card can be the arrival of a miracle you have waited an eternity for which amazingly occurs, though you gave up on it really ever coming true long ago. This trump is synonymous with physical ruin which reflects divine intervention at work transforming the world through natural disaster, futuristic visions of the planet and society and the spiritual law that states all so-called accidents happen for a specific reason and a greater purpose than you can imagine. Also, the Tower urges you to break through hate and separation between groups who attempt to upstage each other with their dogmatic belief code making earth a madhouse leaning further toward the edge on its fall from the heights.

## THE STAR

The Star shows you doing what you were born to do and highlights your highest purpose in life. This can depict you as a spokesperson who educates and enlightens others about a cause or issue through a public position. The Star often symbolizes being well-known in your field or someone entering your life who is famous. In a negative sense, this card can indicate rude, power-hungry people who grab center stage to add another cacophonous voice to the roar of belligerent, egotistical, opinionated idiots who only want to upstage others to hear themselves speak. With the Star, you may find yourself in a position where you can influence others positively toward a certain problem. Due to this responsibility, your behavior is examined or reviewed by those who look to you as a leader or role model.

In a reading, the Star represents being protected from losing direction by your personal guides and your oversoul. These forces push you along a path of experience harmonious to the needs of your inner self. You are given the chance to achieve the ideals you aspire to. Your hopes and dreams are above and beyond what most people want and the birthright of your soul gifts help you to obtain them.

During the time of the Star, you need

to build positivity and light about yourself
to destroy negative thought patterns so
you can reach a higher level of protection,
confidence and experience an increase in
vitality through your entire being. With the
Star, you strive: to affirm your own divinity;
to ride the solar winds of telepathic
communication transmitted between en-
tities; to investigate astrology as a celestial science. This card often sends you on
to planetary travel, the astral plane
and the environment of dreams where
a parallel life connects through laws of
natural attraction by instantaneous
thought.

## THE MOON

The Moon is a psychological card of projecting
fear into your present and your future based
on your past ordeals. The images, thoughts
and feelings that you previously repressed
cause disturbances which overwhelm you.
These trapped emotions result in negative
blocks within the personality and cause
pain, anxiety, weird behavior or psychic
pressure which must be released through
the understanding and awareness of your

conscious mind. It would be excellent for
you to share your anguish with others who
can help you come to terms with these
inner secrets. This will cleanse you of
phobias, delusions, obsessions, addictions
or nightmares which are designed to
lead you to identify why your behavior is
a reaction to what you have forced upon
others in the past. This trump always requires you to expose your soul so you can
beat your karmic condition and reclaim
your true spirit. The Moon symbolizes
the art of psychic healing and the science
of psychoanalysis which explore the workings of the mind. Through utilizing these
disciplines, you can ascertain the state of
your spirit by recreating explosive dramas
from your past which you repeat either
mentally or by attracting partners to
you who substitute for the original person who so powerfully affected your life
long ago.

The Moon has great mystical significance and also rules over creative
art forms including film, music, poetry,
photography, painting, sculpting, writing
and acting. This card is one of exalted
supernatural moments where through a

wordless rapture you receive inspiring dreams, visions or artwork which will be controversial and capable of deeply affecting - even disturbing - your audience.

The Moon is a trump of the collective unconscious, psychics, mystics, hypnotism, animism in the spirit world, obscure mythology, ancient symbolism, prehistoric history and dream interpretation. In the most negative sense it represents: dogmatic groups who cash in on human anxiety by exploiting confused people who are uncertain about exploring the truth of their own spirituality or the world of drugs, alcohol and chemical imbalances of the brain which have the power to turn a happy mood into something ugly pretty fast.

## THE SUN

This card brings a renewal of clarity after the fog and darkness disperse that rolled in with the Moon. The Sun is a liberating card of positive growth, warmth and simplicity of purpose. Its function is to raise your awareness, increase the brilliance of your consciousness and help you to become more certain of your direction in life. You come into peace and safety after struggling through bad times and due to this, you count your blessings and find little to be sad about. With the Sun, you claim your right to serenity and to enjoy your existence as you obtain better conditions for yourself. Because of the fantastic way you feel, you are inspired to give as much as you can to those who cross your path and help them become more content with the reality of their lives.

The Sun is symbolic of creative energy produced by solar wind which all natural forms of being depend on for survival. The supreme power of this star is the source of vital healing rays which up to now in recent history has nurtured growth and change for the ecosystem of the earth. In a reading, this card can move you to a warm climate, sunny environment, the desert, the tropics, travel south or represent the summer months. It assists you in discovering a place that makes you happy where you can enjoy the outdoors during daylight and at night.

Esoterically, this trump describes bright, planetary emanations shining on you from the heavenly spheres, a stage

of opening up in your evolution in consciousness or the afterlife experience where a
golden eternal homeland awaits each soul
between the cycles of rebirth. The Sun is
all-seeing, all-knowing and all-pervasive
and helps us find the supreme good in
ourselves and develop the greatest level
of spirituality possible.

In love, this trump shows a relationship where each partner is the central
force and reason for living for the other.
The joy and contentment of these two
people is renewed whenever they meet
and both are eager to plan a future together. Unity, honesty, monogamy and
integrity mark a union where neither person wants to hurt or lose their most
precious friend.

## JUDGEMENT

This trump applies the rebirth undergone
with the Sun to the concept of universal
history as contained in the akashic records which store data describing the ages
of the past chronicles of the earth and
humankind. Judgement emphasizes the
choices you make before each lifetime

after reviewing the entire spectrum of your behavior to ascertain how you can fulfill your debt and reap the bounty of karmic reward. Your oversoul is the part of you that is completely aware of your history and plans a future designed to balance out extreme or negative personality traits from former incarnations. You select themes and issues to confront that will enable you to pay your dues and clear your slate without generating more destructive behavior to contend with later on.

All lives past, present and yet to come are ruled by Judgement. The common thread that runs through your eternity shows you seeking a role that will synchronize with the evolution of your soul. During thoughts of "Why me?" and "Why can't I?", try to comprehend why these prearranged crises are perfect stepping stones for your personal growth. You should think in terms of infinity how every act ultimately determines how rapidly you progress on your journey to the stars and serving the universe. This trump urges you to remove yourself from negative places, people and situations and shift yourself to becoming more spiritually responsible for your work, your relationships and your life style.

## THE UNIVERSE

The Universe represents the end of a period of time as a major turning point for you where a stage of completion is reached in the cycle in which you are working. Each soul moves with the clock of the natural world connected to it by the mantra of the heartbeat in all galaxies which comprise the infinite cosmos. With this trump, you become aware of the multisteps in growth and evolution which lead you closer to your reunion with the divine source of all creation. The spiritual surrender begun with the Fool and developed through the experiences of the previous twenty-one trumps moves you into alignment with your true self who realizes the value and importance of returning to earth to take care of unfinished business.

In a reading, the Universe says everything is as it should be and anything that seems like a waste of time and energy is really a precious gift of leisure to explore the significance of the past as it relates to your present sojourn. Any delays will lead you to an improved position ultimately through a slow but eventual change of fortune. Let providence provide for you and do not fight the inevitable by attempting to control the natural unfolding of your destiny. After your karmic blocks explode through the force of recalling your past behavior, you meet the fate that will bring you the most happiness and a sense of an exalted purpose for your life. You recognize your celestial origin and comprehend why you have come back to earth at this time to meet with like-minded people and together work positively for a renewed future.

The Universe symbolizes cosmic force as it enters the sphere of earth through the energy of the planets, the stars, the elements, all spiritual beings and all forms of universal creation. This card describes the outreach of space which contains the vastness of all eternity. The silent power of the harmony of the spheres shows the way of heaven and the movement of each soul toward perfection of the spirit. Astrologically, this card depicts the microcosmic human being in exact relationship to the macrocosmic universe and its laws of change and continuity. With the final trump, you fulfill the blueprint of your natal chart where the big picture of your true potential can be understood symbolically. The Universe signifies the importance of there being a balance between the earth and the individual who decides to take responsibility for the planet through a correct life style arrangement which enables them to meet their destiny and concurrently respect all manifestations of the cosmic life force.

# EXERCISES IN SYNTHESIZING
# THE MEANINGS OF THE TAROT CARDS

# CARD COMBINATIONS AND THEIR MEANINGS

ACE OF DISKS and SEVEN OF DISKS: have patience and let the issue of the reading develop in a slow, proper manner.

EIGHT OF WANDS and KNIGHT OF SWORDS: shows the need to get things together quickly.

KING OF SWORDS and KING OF CUPS: both love to play the controlling ruler who withholds information.

THE JUGGLER and THE DEVIL: there is more than meets the eye in an atmosphere thick with peculiar occurrences.

SEVEN OF SWORDS and KING OF CUPS: shows entrepreneurship.

SIX OF SWORDS and SIX OF WANDS: indicates a major breakthrough.

TWO OF SWORDS and TWO OF DISKS: watching and waiting.

THE MOON and THE SUN: like an eclipse, the energy of these two planets struggle with each other as your experience of water and memory combines with your experience of fire and clarity.

FOUR OF WANDS and JUPITER: contentment on a very high level.

NINE OF CUPS and THE FOOL: happiness

and emotional security which come as a surprise.

THREE, SIX and NINE OF DISKS: finally getting paid for work completed.

EIGHT OF DISKS, NINE OF DISKS and THE JUGGLER: to practically apply the abilities over which you have gained mastery.

FIVE OF SWORDS and EIGHT OF SWORDS: feeling hung up and vulnerable about communicating with another person.

ACE OF WANDS and THREE OF WANDS: Says that you can handle what is happening.

FIVE OF CUPS and JUPITER: the highest level of romantic love and friendship.

PAGE OF SWORDS and ACE OF WANDS: you have a very powerful guardian angel who uses a club to wake you up and move you on to new experiences.

STRENGTH and JUDGEMENT: a strong decision based on correct and courageous behavior.

ACE OF DISKS and THE FOOL: things dropping out of nowhere.

JUNO and THE EMPRESS: connecting with the Goddess in yourself.

TWO OF DISKS and THREE OF DISKS: to need to travel for completion of a project.

SEVEN OF DISKS and EIGHT OF DISKS: working
  diligently and patiently toward perfection
  of a talent or artwork and completely
  immersing yourself in this activity.
FIVE and SEVEN OF SWORDS and SEVEN
  OF WANDS: fighting for your independence.
TWO OF DISKS and JUDGEMENT: though nothing appears to be happening, major decisions are being made anyway.
ACE OF WANDS and KING OF WANDS: exercising the right to be good or a good man
  who helps you get the ball rolling.
FIVE OF DISKS and JUPITER: leading a
  more spiritual life or adopting a
  charitable outlook.
EIGHT OF DISKS and THREE OF CUPS:
  celebration over your ability, creativity,
  expertise and industry.
ACE OF CUPS and THE WHEEL OF FORTUNE:
  you are jubilant about a love affair
  and feel lucky and blessed to have found
  a wonderful person.
TWO OF SWORDS and FIVE OF CUPS: the tension that arises from not having a relationship, which only wastes your energy.
JUSTICE, THE HANGED MAN and JUDGE-
  MENT: tests and trials which help you
  define the purpose of your existence,

DEATH and THE MOON: You are going through
an overwhelmingly difficult time of
change, purging and purification.
PAGE OF WANDS and KING OF WANDS:
you can expect total reliability through
the male support system in your life.
THE EMPEROR and JUPITER: lots of heavy,
influential male energy around you.
SEVEN OF DISKS and SEVEN OF WANDS:
trying hard to be patient.
EIGHT OF DISKS and NINE OF WANDS:
building up security.
THREE OF DISKS and NINE OF DISKS: your
skills and talents have been recognized by others.
TEN OF CUPS and KNIGHT OF CUPS: you sense
that a certain relationship has the
potential to grow into a deep, satisfying
union but you are unsure of the other
person's true intentions.
EIGHT OF CUPS and JUPITER: get back
to spiritual devotion.
THE LOVERS and SEVEN OF SWORDS:
a romance when, where and how you
want it.
NINE OF SWORDS and STRENGTH: painful lessons which empower you.
EIGHT OF CUPS and FIVE OF WANDS:

something captures you passionately,
heart and soul.

ACE OF CUPS and PAGE OF CUPS: being
gentle and nice.

KING OF DISKS and THE EMPEROR: those
who are concerned about your welfare
and help you out unselfishly and practically.

THE HANGED MAN and THE STAR: being in
the spotlight as a result of your beliefs.

ACE OF CUPS and ACE OF SWORDS: open
heart, open mind.

TWO OF CUPS and PAGE OF SWORDS: information coming to you that is loving
and makes you happy.

FIVE OF CUPS and THE UNIVERSE: though
you know you're on the right path, you
are overwhelmed by an emotional disappointment that leaves you unfulfilled.

SIX OF DISKS and THREE OF CUPS: sharing pleasure and your riches with others.

THE HERMIT and TEMPERANCE: the need
to spend time alone to work out the
rough edges of your personality.

THE LOVERS and JUSTICE: working
out a marriage agreement or breaking your vows or divorce, depending
upon the nature of the reading.

# TAROT CARDS WITH SIMILAR MEANINGS

CARDS OF SELF-DEFENSE: eight and King of swords; King of cups; five, seven and nine of wands; the Juggler.

CARDS OF SELF-RELIANCE: five, seven and King of swords; King of cups; two of wands; the Hermit and Strength.

CARDS OF THINKING FOR YOURSELF: ace, two, five, seven and Page through King of swords; the Juggler, Juno, Justice, the Hermit, the Hanged Man and Judgement.

CARDS OF CHOICE: ace, four and five of swords; the Lovers, Justice, the Hanged Man, the Devil and Judgement.

CARDS OF GOING YOUR OWN WAY: seven of swords; eight of cups; seven of wands; the Hermit and the Hanged Man.

CARDS OF INTELLIGENCE: all the sword people and the six and ten of swords; the Juggler, Juno and Jupiter.

CARDS OF AUTHORITY: all Kings; the Juggler,

Juno, the Emperor, Jupiter, Justice and the Hanged Man.

**CARDS OF TEACHERS:** King of swords; King of wands; Juno, Jupiter and the Hanged Man.

**CARDS OF STUDENTS:** ace of disks; eight of cups; all the Pages.

**CARDS OF LEADERS:** Knight of swords and seven of swords; King of cups; King of disks; five and seven of wands; the Juggler, Juno, the Empress, the Emperor, Jupiter, the Hermit and the Hanged Man.

**CARDS OF QUIET, INTROSPECTION AND SOLITUDE:** four of swords; Knight of disks; eight and King of cups; the Juggler, Juno, the Hermit and the Hanged Man.

**CARDS OF COMING INTO CLARITY:** six, eight and ace of swords; six of cups; the Hanged Man, Death, the Devil, the Tower, the Sun and Judgement.

**CARDS OF INSPIRATION:** six of swords;

six, seven and eight of cups; eight of wands; Juno, the Empress, the Star and the Sun.

CARDS OF BEAUTY: Page of cups; Temperance, the Star, the Sun, the Moon and the Universe.

CARDS OF VISUALIZATION: two and Page of swords; seven of cups; Juno and the Moon.

CARDS OF INTUITION: two and four of swords; eight and Queen of cups; the Fool, the Juggler, Jupiter, the Hermit, the Hanged Man, Temperance and the Sun.

CARDS OF FAITH: two of swords; the Fool, Juno, the Hermit, the Wheel of Fortune and the Universe.

CARDS OF SPIRITUAL DEVOTION: two and four of swords; Knight of disks; eight, Page and Queen of cups; Page of wands; the Fool, the Juggler, Juno, Jupiter, the Hermit, the Hanged Man, Temperance the Sun and the Universe.

CARDS OF OPENING UP TO GUIDANCE:
eight and Page of swords; the Fool, the
Juggler, Juno, Jupiter, the Chariot,
the Wheel of Fortune, the Tower, the
Star and the Universe.

CARDS OF PURIFICATION: ace of wands;
the Hermit, Strength, the Hanged Man,
Death, Temperance, the Devil, the
Tower and the Moon.

CARDS OF REBIRTH: ace of wands; the
Fool and the entire force and function
of the other twenty-one trumps.

CARDS OF PAST LIFE ABILITY: ten of
swords; ace of disks; Juno, Jupiter,
Justice, the Wheel of Fortune and the
Universe.

CARDS OF BALANCE AND EQUILIBRIUM:
two of swords; two of disks; the Empress,
the Emperor, Justice, the Hermit, Strength,
the Hanged Man, the Star and Judgement.

CARDS OF HARMONY: all sixes; ace, two,
three, six, nine and ten of cups; the
Lovers, Justice, the Wheel of Fortune,

Temperance, the Star and the Universe.

CARDS OF RENEWAL: six of cups; ace of wands; Death, the Tower, Temperance, the Star and the Sun.

CARDS OF PHYSICAL WELL-BEING: three and nine of cups; four of wands; Strength and Temperance and the Sun.

CARDS OF GENEROSITY: ace, two, six, nine, ten and all disk court cards; six and Queen of cups.

CARDS OF CELEBRATION: ace, two, three, six nine, ten and Knight of cups; four and six of wands; the Wheel of Fortune.

CARDS OF ECSTASY: ace, three, seven and ten of cups; ace and eight of wands; the Fool, the Lovers, the Tower (in its most positive sense), the Star and the Sun.

CARDS OF FRIENDSHIP: three, four, five, Page and Queen of cups; four and Page of wands; the Sun.

**CARDS OF DEVOTION:** Knight and King of disks; the Pages disk, cup and wand; eight of cups; King of wands; the Lovers, the Hanged Man, Temperance and the Sun.

**CARDS OF HAPPINESS:** ace, two, three, six, nine and ten of cups; four and six of wands; the Fool, the Chariot, the Wheel of Fortune, the Star and the Sun.

**CARDS OF DEEP CARING:** ace, two, three, six, eight, ten, Page and Queen of cups; three of swords; nine, Queen, Knight and King of disks; all wands; the Empress, the Emperor, the Lovers, Jupiter, Strength, the Sun and the Star.

**CARDS OF TRUE LOVE:** ace, two, six, nine and ten of cups; six of wands; Jupiter, the Lovers and the Sun.

**CARDS OF PASSIONATE LOVE:** ace, two, three, four, five, six, eight, nine, ten, Page, Queen, Knight and King of wands; two, three, nine and ten of cups; the Lovers, Strength and the Sun.

**CARDS OF SPIRITUAL LOVE:** ace, two, three, eight, nine, ten and Page of cups; the Juggler, Juno, Jupiter, the Lovers, the Hermit, the Hanged Man, Temperance, the Star, the Moon and the Sun.

**CARDS OF CHALLENGING LOVE RELATIONSHIPS:** three, five and nine of swords; four and five of cups; five, seven and ten of wands; the Knights sword, cup and wand; the Kings sword and cup.

**CARDS OF TRUTH:** ace, two, seven, nine and King of swords; ace, five, Page and King of wands; the Fool, the Juggler, Juno, Jupiter, Justice, the Hermit, Strength, the Hanged Man, Death, the Tower, the Sun, Judgement and the Universe.

**CARDS OF HONEST, FAITHFUL PEOPLE:** King of swords; all disk court cards; Page and King of wands; Page of cups; the Empress, the Emperor, the Hermit, Jupiter and the Hanged Man.

**CARDS OF ACTIVISM:** five, seven and

Page of swords; eight of cups; two, five
and seven of wands; the Fool, Jupiter,
the Hanged Man and the Star.

CARDS OF LIBERATION: ace, six, seven
and eight of swords; ace and six of
wands; the Fool, Justice, the Wheel of
Fortune, Strength, the Hanged Man,
Death, the Tower and the Universe.

CARDS OF GREAT FORCE: ace of swords;
ace, two, eight and nine of wands;
the Juggler, the Chariot, the Wheel of
Fortune, Strength, Death, the Tower,
the Sun, Judgement and the Universe.

CARDS OF INTENSE ACTIVITY: six, Page
and Knight of swords; eight of disks;
seven of cups; all wands, especially
the ace, five, seven, eight, ten and
Knight.

CARDS OF SKILL DEVELOPMENT: three,
four, six, seven, eight, nine, ten and
Page of disks; the Emperor, Temperance
and the Star.

CARDS OF COMPLETION OF WORK:

three, eight and ten of disks; ten of swords;
three and six of wands; the Emperor,
Temperance, Judgement and the Universe.

CARDS OF MONEY: ace, three, four, five,
six, nine, ten, Queen and King of disks;
the Wheel of Fortune and the Emperor.

CARDS OF SECURITY: four, six, nine, ten
and Page-King of disks; seven, nine
and King of wands; the Empress, the
Emperor, the Chariot and the Wheel
of Fortune.

CARDS OF RISK TAKING: two, five, seven,
Page and Knight of swords; ace, two,
five, six, seven, eight and Knight of
wands; the Fool, the Juggler and the
Wheel of Fortune.

CARDS OF SURPRISE: ace and eight of
wands; the Fool, Death and the Tower.

CARDS OF ENDURANCE: three, four, seven,
eight, nine and ten of disks; eight
and ten of cups; all disk court cards;
the Empress, the Emperor, Strength,
Temperance, Judgement and the Universe.

**CARDS OF PATIENCE:** all aces; two and eight of swords; seven and eight of disks; eight of cups; nine of wands; the Chariot, Temperance and the Universe.

**CARDS OF DORMANCY:** ace, two and seven of disks; eight of swords; the Chariot, Death and Temperance.

**CARDS OF NEW BEGINNINGS:** all aces; the Fool, Death and the Tower.

**CARDS OF THE PASSAGE OF TIME:** two of disks; the Chariot, the Wheel of Fortune, Temperance and the Universe.

**CARDS OF GREAT SPEED:** aces of sword and wand; six of swords; eight of wands; Knights of sword and wand; the Chariot and the Wheel of Fortune.

**CARDS OF RETREAT:** four and Knight of swords; Knight of wands; the Hermit and the Hanged Man.

**CARDS OF CONFUSION:** five, seven, eight, nine, ten and Knight of swords; four, five, seven and Knight of cups; two of disks;

eight and ten of wands; the Devil, the Tower and the Moon.

CARDS OF LACK OF FREE WILL: two, eight and Page of swords; the Chariot, Justice and the Hanged Man.

CARDS OF NONPRODUCTIVE HABITS: Knights of sword, cup and wand; four and five of cups; the Devil.

CARDS OF WASTED TALENT: three, eight, nine and ten of swords; five of disks; five and Knight of cups; five and ten of wands; the Devil.

CARDS OF BEING ALONE: three, four, nine, ten and Queen and King of swords; five, eight and King of cups; the Hermit, the Hanged Man, Temperance and Judgement.

CARDS OF DEPRESSION: three, eight, nine and ten of swords; the Devil and the Moon.

CARDS OF PAIN: three, nine and ten of swords; five and Page of cups; Death and the Devil.

CARDS OF SORROW: three, four, eight, nine, ten and Queen of swords; five and eight of cups; the Hermit, the Hanged Man, Death and the Devil.

CARDS OF ILLUSION: seven, Queen, Knight and King of cups; the Juggler, the Devil, the Tower and the Moon.

PLANETARY CARDS: the Wheel of Fortune, the Star, the Moon, the Sun and the Universe.

CARDS OF THE EARTH: all disks, especially the nine, two, Queen and Knight; the Empress, Juno, the Wheel of Fortune, Death and the Universe (also called the World).

# TEN NEW TAROT SPREADS

## TEN NEW TAROT SPREADS

These spreads, new to readers of <u>The Tarot</u>,
do not require you to identify the significa-
tor or ascertain the subject-combination.
Simply take your Tarot deck into your hands
and shuffle the deck three times. Then lay
the cards out face down in the spread positions according to their numerical order,
drawing cards from the top of the shuffled
deck.

    Try to keep the cards going in the
same direction when you shuffle the deck.
If the cards become a mixture of right
side up and reversed (upside-down), turn
them right side up to face you as they
are turned over, one by one, as you interpret the spread.

    When you have fully reviewed the
spread to your satisfaction, gather all
the cards back together and repeat the
shuffling process if you wish to continue
on to other Tarot spreads.

## ASTROLOGICAL SPREADS

There are three different ways to utilize the following layout of twelve

cards.

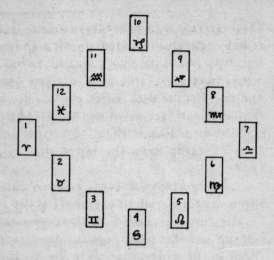

As a forecast for the year ahead of
you, you would do this spread only once
a year with card number one symbolizing
the month you are in at the time of the
reading. Place one card down on each
of the following eleven placements
which correspond to the remaining months.
Record this reading so you can refer to
it monthly to see how the Tarot card for
each month represents the lessons, activities and people that will dominate your
life during that period of time.

The second method of application for this spread would emphasize your natal astrological chart. Again, place one card down on each of the twelve positions. This time each card would illustrate the twelve houses of the horoscope, card number one corresponding to the first house, card number two corresponding to the second house and so on. The Tarot card which appears in the house placement of the reading symbolizes the nature of your experience and involvement with the area of life defined by the twelve house system of the science of astrology. For those unfamiliar with the meanings of the houses, here are the following definitions for you to use when you employ this second method.

| HOUSE | MEANING |
|-------|---------|
| first | your physical appearance and outward personality; the way you move, act and the vibration you send out through the expressions of your face and body. |
| second | your resources, talents and abilities; your experience of personal |

| HOUSE | MEANING |
|---|---|
| second (cont.) | values; your sense of responsibility; your ability to attract money and possessions to yourself. |
| third | short journeys; early life conditions, especially your environment, relatives and neighbors and their influence on you; the condition of your conscious mind; your communication skills and your exposure to knowledge. |
| fourth | the more passive of your parents; your home and property; your self-image and sense of security. |
| fifth | your love life, children, personal pleasure, enjoyment, entertainment, self-expression and creativity; speculation and risk taking. |
| sixth | your physical needs and domestic environment; conflict as it affects your health or employment; your ability to serve others. |

| HOUSE | MEANING |
|-------|---------|
| seventh | people who you are in relationship with as a partner whether through marriage or business; those who oppose you as enemies or antagonists. |
| eighth | death; legacies both psychic brought over from other lives and those inherited materially in this life; joint resources; sensuality; parapsychology. |
| ninth | long journeys and foreign lands and people; higher education; philosophical interests; the superconscious mind: visions, dreams and symbolism. |
| tenth | your more active parent; career direction, reputation and public image that define your outer life works and pathway. |
| eleventh | friendships and social life; long-term goals and objectives; humanitarianism; the future. |

| HOUSE | MEANING |
|-------|---------|
| twelfth | your tendency to hide things from others; your need for privacy and secrecy; your limitations, frustrations and confinements; the state of your soul in terms of karmic troubles; your subconscious mind; initiation into the mysteries and spiritual perfection. |

The third way to use this layout is by applying the twelve card arrangement to a very abstract and advanced spread which analyzes energy and matter as influenced by the forces of the natural world.

The twelve cards this time correspond to the twelve signs of the zodiac which have rulership over the twelve houses of the astrological chart. In the following chart, the houses connect with a zodiac sign which in turn has a symbol in quadruplicate elemental energies of earth, air, fire, water as combined and manifested in a creative or atmospheric force found in nature:

| HOUSE AND SIGN | COMBINED ENERGY OF | FORCE |
| --- | --- | --- |
| first/Aries | earth of fire | rays |
| second/Taurus | earth of air | silence |
| third/Gemini | water of air | song |
| fourth/Cancer | fire of water | steam |
| fifth/Leo | air of fire | lightning |
| sixth/Virgo | air of earth | dust |
| seventh/Libra | air of water | mist |
| eighth/Scorpio | water of earth | mud |
| ninth/Sagittarius | water of fire | flame |
| tenth/Capricorn | fire of earth | crystal |
| eleventh/Aquarius | fire of air | thunder |
| twelfth/Pisces | earth of water | rain |

# ELEMENTAL SPREAD

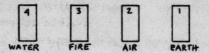

| 4 | 3 | 2 | 1 |
| WATER | FIRE | AIR | EARTH |

To utilize this spread, lay the top four cards out in the four placements above and interpret the cards from right to left.

Each of the elements has the following correspondence to the four suits of the Tarot and generates the following activities in your life.

| ELEMENT | SUIT | ACTIVITIES |
| --- | --- | --- |
| earth | disk | the body and all physical sensation; material expression of spirit in matter; money, talent and constructive building up of practical ability. |
| air | sword | the mind, thought and intellect; plan or realization; communication; decisions. |
| fire | wand | passion and desire; |

| ELEMENT | SUIT | ACTIVITIES |
|---------|------|------------|
| fire (cont.) | wand | creative force; the spirit in action; life giving energy; what you strive for and believe in. |
| water | cup | the subconscious mind; soul qualities; receptivity, imagination and visualization; what a situation puts you through emotionally. |

## THE CHAKTRA SPREAD

Chaktras are spinning wheels of energy centered in seven areas of the internal physical body through which different areas and levels of nonphysical qualities of humanity are expressed. Negative emotions and actions and thoughts create blocks in any or all of the chaktras which are karmic in origin and need to be identified and healed until perfect alignment and free-flowing consciousness is achieved.

This spread utilizes seven cards,

each representing one of the chaktras. Read it from bottom to top and apply the following definitions to the appropriate chaktra.

7. **CROWN CHAKTRA:** superconscious mind; connection to divine source; to be at one with the universe; reunion with Godhead.

6. **THIRD EYE CHAKTRA:** extrasensory perception; imagination; creativity; to use more of your brain, memory and subconscious mind.

5. **THROAT CHAKTRA:** expression and communication; information from higher mind; what you have to say.

4. **HEART CHAKTRA:** love experiences in your life; your ability to trust others and open up your heart to them.

3. **SOLAR PLEXUS CHAKTRA:** self-confidence; the power of relaxation; nurturance; centeredness; female fertility.

2. **SEX CHAKTRA:** desire; animal nature; instinct; your emotional response to life.

1. **ROOT CHAKTRA:** earthly physical needs and requirements; how you deal with realities of existence; your conscious mind; your survival instinct.

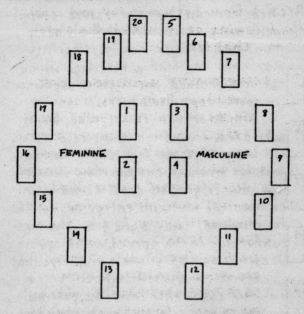

This layout examines the stages of development in your relationships with those of the opposite sex in terms of karma brought forth from your childhood experience (cards 1, 2, 3 and 4) with your parents, guardians or figures of love and authority and how this has influenced your subconscious self-image. Implied in this spread (cards 5-20) is the pathway to your ideal person or soul mate with whom you can share a mature commitment without repeating as an adult the identical union that your parents may have and find a marriage which reflects instead the highest aspirations for your deeply loving self.

To interpret this spread, begin with cards 1 and 2 which indicate your self-image if you are female. The Tarot cards that fall in these two positions show the way you see yourself due to karma taken on from the maternal energy in your life. For a woman, cards 3 and 4 on the masculine side of the spread would symbolize your animus or male archetype that you attract to yourself naturally based on your experience with the paternal energy in your life which has played a large role in your self-esteem level. Cards 1 through 4 show the karma taken on by a female through her parents, good or bad.

For a man, cards 3 and 4 on the masculine side of the spread would indicate your self-image as a man due to karma taken on from the fatherly influence in your life. Cards 1 and 2 would describe your anima or female archetype you unconsciously seek based on your experiences with feminine energy. If you have already made the release of any negativity inherited through the influence of the parents, cards 1 to 4 would take on a higher meaning and be more indicative of a search for the highest, purest complementary soul mate and would show a man animating cards 3 and 4 in his most spiritual manner and finding his true consort through the activities of the cards which surface in positions 1 and 2. This would apply vice versa for a woman reading her cards.

For a female, cards 5 through 12 symbolize what her man has to accomplish psychologically, emotionally, spiritually and materially on his path to meeting her and through the early stages of the relationship with card 12 defining the nature of the union in its outcome. Cards 13-20 show her what she has to go through in her experience until she is secure with her connection to the right man (card 20).

For a man, cards 13-20 depict what

his soul mate is going through to find
him and at what level her male archetype is at. Cards 5-12 show him on his
path to one true love.

## AS ABOVE, SO BELOW

This directional spread examines the
forces that surround you and influence
your movement and position in life.

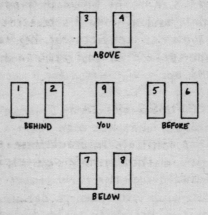

To use this spread, lay the top nine cards
out in the layout illustrated above. Cards
1 and 2 symbolize the past, what is behind
you, over and done with and is losing
its power and influence over your life.

Cards 3 and 4 describe what crowns you, is above you, environmental factors affecting you and how you merge with society. Cards 5 and 6 have to do with what is before you in your future, what is ahead of you, the outcome of the subject matter of the reading and what is growing more dominant along the horizon of life yet to come. Cards 7 and 8 show what is below or beneath you, what you already have under control and the forces of support that exist for you. Card 9 represents you, the inquirer, and depicts the central core experience that you undergo in this reading.

## LIFETIMES SPREAD

Eight cards are laid out from left to right in this simple self-explanatory spread.

This spread should not be done too often and should be recorded for future reference.

## THREE CARD SPREAD

This is a quick spread designed to answer the most specific of questions posed to the deck in the least amount of time.

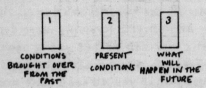

Read from left to right, interpreting card 1 as conditions brought over from the past affecting the issue brought to the reading, card 2 as present conditions and card 3 as the outcome of the matter or the direction your involvement will take depending upon the nature of the Tarot card that surfaces there.

## PROBLEM/SOLUTION SPREAD

This layout helps you get to the heart of the reasons as to why certain difficult experiences happen for a purpose in your life. It analyzes how you can first identify the nature of the problem and deal with it through positive action to resolve this old issue your soul has chosen to deal with at the time of the reading.

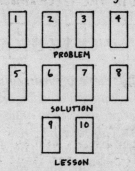

The ten cards are laid out in the above arrangement. Cards 1 through 4 symbolize the current status of the issue, focusing on the problem that you face. Cards 5 through 8 show you what course of action will lead to a satisfying solution to the situation. Cards 9 and 10 depict the karmic lesson inherent in this obstacle which once realized can change the course of your life pathway.

355